100

pin loom
SQUARES

A Quantum Book

First published in the UK in 2015 by
Apple Press
74–77 White Lion Street
London N1 9PF
United Kingdom

www.apple-press.com

ISBN 978-1-84543-558-5

QUMEAPL

This book was conceived,
designed and produced by

Quantum Books Limited
6 Blundell Street
London N7 9BH
United Kingdom

Publisher: Kerry Enzor
Project Editor: Hazel Eriksson
Editor: Julie Brooke
Designers: Mark Hudson and Gareth Butterworth
Photographer: Simon Pask
Project Photography (pages 106–138): Osvaldo Faúndez
Technical Consultants: Emma Brace, Catherine Embleton
and Sophie Scott
Production Manager: Rohana Yusof

Printed in China by 1010 Printing International Ltd.

9 8 7 6 5 4 3 2 1

100
pin loom
SQUARES

Florencia Campos Correa

APPLE

Contents

Foreword

I've always loved creating things, and fabrics have been my means of expression for many years. I started in the traditional way, watching my mom and grandma weaving, and then improvising with my own fabrics to dress my dolls; making colourful woven, handmade Christmas gifts; and also venturing timidly into business by selling my creations to my family and friends.

I believe my fascination with weaving comes from the countless possibilities it gives you – by simply weaving yarn you can build incredible, three-dimensional shapes. Fabrics offer an endless versatility, more so if you are able to combine the strengths of different techniques: weaving, crochet, felting, beading and embroidery. The truth is that the only limit is your imagination.

I studied Industrial Design at a time in my life when weaving was just a childhood memory. When I picked it up again later in life it allowed me to combine my education and profession with a mixture of creativity and resourcefulness.

Now, I don't consider myself a professional weaver, I just like to experiment. So I decided to try pin-loom weaving. My mom taught me to use the triangle loom and out of curiosity I started to try the same technique on other geometric shapes, by building my own looms from spare pieces of wood.

I am convinced that you get better results by always experimenting with yarns and colours and this book is geared to help you create your own unique designs.

Each technique in this book is described using easy-to-follow steps that will enable you to master the basics of hand-loom weaving. The rest of the journey is a personal one, where the true, therapeutic art of weaving starts. Therefore, my invitation is for you to experiment and surprise yourself; to relax and let your creativity flow. It is truly rewarding to make something that pleases other people as well as yourself, so much so that they ask you if they can keep it or buy it. That is the happiest moment of the entire process. It doesn't matter how many times it happens, almost every time will feel like the first – you will feel a sense of indescribable gratitude.

How to Use This Book

If you are new to weaving with the Zoom Loom and other pin looms, the Getting Started section (see pages 10–19) contains invaluable information about weaving. The Setting up the Loom and Weaving Techniques chapter (see pages 20–53) explains all the basic techniques you need to know. You'll then be inspired by the Gallery of Squares (see pages 54–105) and Creative Projects (see pages 106–139).

Find out how to set up your loom

The first step is to set up the warp threads so they are ready for weaving. There are two ways to do this: the two-layer warp thread setup (see pages 38–39) and the three-layer warp thread setup (see pages 22–24).

Weaving techniques explained

Once you have set up the warp threads it's time to weave the weft threads. This book contains 22 weft-thread patterns.

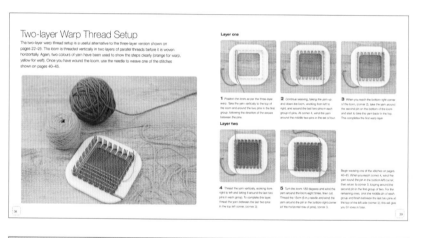

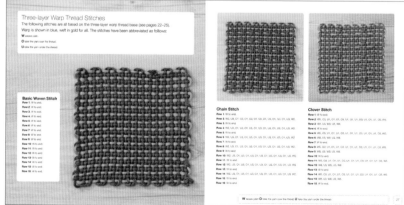

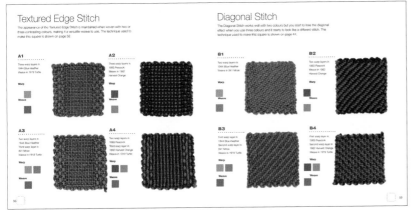

Lots of colours and stitches

The joy of weaving on pin looms such as the Zoom Loom is that you can quickly create fabric squares using combinations of colours and weft thread patterns. The Gallery of Squares (see pages 54–105) will give you 100 ideas for effects you can achieve.

Projects to try

Once you have woven your squares you will want to show them off. The simplest way is to use them as a set of coasters. But if you're looking to make a statement with them, the fifteen projects shown here will inspire you.

Abbreviations

The weft-thread patterns in this book are abbreviated in the same way that a knitting or crochet pattern might be. However, unlike those crafts, there are only three codes to remember:

W weave plain.
O take the yarn over the thread.
U take the yarn under the thread.

Getting Started

Pin looms are the perfect tool for those who want to try their hand at weaving. Once you have mastered the basic woven stitch (see page 26) it should take about 15 minutes to weave a square. This makes pin-loom weaving a quick, satisfying way to create your own luxurious and colourful fabrics and experiment with them.

The squares can be woven from a single colour or type of yarn, or you can experiment by mixing up the colours and yarns to create new colour and texture effects by tying in different yarns whenever you like.

The History of Pin-loom Weaving

The 1930s saw a craze for weaving on hand-held looms and transforming the resulting squares into anything from a place mat to an afghan, baby's hat or woman's jacket. Dozens of manuals and pattern books showed new converts to the craft how to weave different patterns into their squares and then sew or crochet them together to make garments and accessories.

It is likely that the outbreak of the Second World War brought about the end of the boom in weaving on these small wooden or plastic looms set with a series of metal pins or wooden pegs. However, the Weave-It loom – which was one of the most popular and was patented in 1934 – continued to be made into the early 1970s.

The Weave-It has a three-pin arrangement, which makes it very easy to wrap the yarn around and is used as the basis for some modern looms. In the 1930s, the design was used on early versions of the Loomette, which went on sale in 1935, although it was soon replaced by a loom with evenly spaced pins and a system of metal bars which enabled the user to make smaller squares and rectangles on the loom.

Another variation was the Magic Loom by Bucilla, which has pins at different heights to facilitate easy weaving.

The earliest pin looms to use were probably made by Easiweave, but others from the 1930s include Jiffy-Looms, Double Weeve, Davis Loom, Hollywood, Auto-Weave, Simplex, Pucki and Le Tissor.

You may have an old loom at the back of a cupboard, or it is possible to buy vintage looms from charity or antique shops, at jumble sales, or online. Don't worry if you don't have the instruction booklet – use the instructions in this book to start weaving, look in charity shops for original copies, or online for facsimiles of them. You will also need a long needle (15cm/6 in. is usual) for weaving and a 7.5cm (3 in.) needle for sewing in ends and sewing the squares together. You can usually buy these in craft shops or online.

If you're buying a vintage loom, make sure no pins are missing or broken and that the frame is not warped. Both of these will prevent you using the loom. A little rust on the pins can be cleaned off but check plastic looms do not have a strong chemical smell – if they do the plastic may be degrading and should be avoided at all costs.

The Loom

Small hand-held looms are eminently portable, and the easy-to-handle frames often feature markings to help guide you when winding the warp threads and weaving the weft. Most looms will come supplied with the 15cm (6 in.) and 7.5cm (3 in.) needles you need to weave and sew the squares. The only other equipment you will need is a pair of scissors, a tape measure and – if you want to crochet your squares together – a crochet hook.

Pin looms can be used to create fabrics with varying degrees of drape depending on the yarns used (see page 50) and the method of laying the warp threads on the loom.

The frame of the Schacht Zoom Loom is marked with numbers and arrows to guide you as you weave. These markings can be added to other looms as per the template supplied on page 18. Hold the frame and use the sloping edge to help guide the needle as you weave.

This book includes instructions for a number of different stitches (see pages 26–47) to enable you to explore the art of weaving, but do not be confined by these – use them as a starting point to create your own.

The woven squares can be sewn or crocheted together (see pages 48–49) to create garments and accessories. These are likely to be symmetrical thanks to the design of the woven stitches and are ideal for blankets, scarves, jackets and bags.

Once you are comfortable making your squares, check out the project section of this book for great ideas – and then start coming up with unique project ideas all of your own! Have a think about what you want to make with your woven squares before beginning; this will dictate your yarn and colour choices and also give you an idea of how many squares you will need.

The great thing about pin-loom weaving is that there are no major rules or technical things to worry about – just follow the basic instructions and practice a few times until you feel confident and then you can improvise to your heart's content.

Building Your Own Loom

Recycle square wooden picture frames or other strips of wood to make your first pin loom. Alternatively, buy new wood from any home supply store. The frame is the least important aspect of the loom, however; the pin placement is what's really important. Use the template on page 18 as your guide to placing the pins.

To make a 10-cm (4-in.) loom

You will need

4 lengths of wood 12.5cm (5 in.) long by 2.5cm (1 in.) wide

2 lengths of wood 7.5cm (3 in.) long by 2.5cm (1 in.) wide

Wood glue

109 (2cm/¾ in.) lost head nails – it's a good idea to have some extras in case you accidentally bend a few. (If your wooden strips are thick, you may find it easier to use 4cm/1½ in. lost head nails.)

Hammer

Pencil

Tape measure or ruler

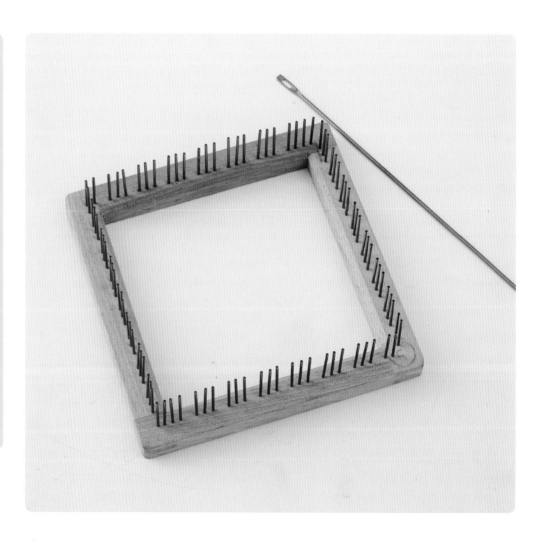

Making the loom

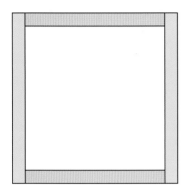 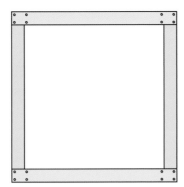 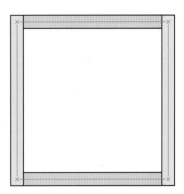

1 On a flat work surface, position two long and two short strips of wood as shown above. Use wood glue to stick all four pieces together. The side nearest to you will be the front of the loom.

2 Lay the remaining two strips along the top and bottom of the loom, as shown. Hammer in 4 nails in each corner. This gives the frame the necessary structure. Sand the wood to make the loom comfortable to hold.

3 Turn the loom over to mark the placement of the nails. Mark the centre of the corners with an 'x' and gently draw a line from corner to corner to create 4 lines.

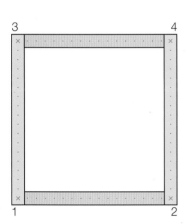 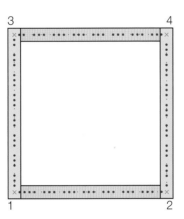 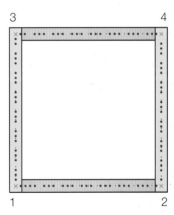

4 Write the numbers 1–4 in the corners as shown. Divide the space between the 'x' marks into 31 equal parts. If a mark is on, or close to, the edge of the wood move it a few millimetres; this will not affect the weaving. The pins are closer to the inside edges – this makes the loom more comfortable to use.

5 Using the template on page 18 as a guide, indicate the marks which will have nails. Note that the 'x' marks in corners 1 and 3 do not have nails, while those in corners 2 and 4 do. Alternatively, copy and cut out the template and tape it to your frame to give you the correct nail placement.

6 Now you have the necessary marks for nailing the 93 pins you will need to weave. Hammer in the nails until at least one-third of the nail is in the wood and try to keep the heads of the nails at the same level where possible.

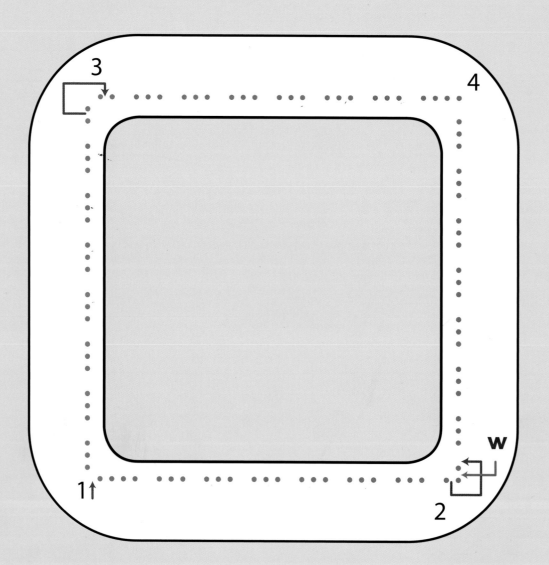

Making a Larger Loom

By increasing the size of the frame but keeping pin placement proportionate, you can make a larger loom to make larger squares. These are great for working with bulkier yarns. Or you can make a smaller loom to make smaller squares with fine yarns.

Loom size is measured on the nail placement lines; this also indicates the size of the squares the loom will produce. Simply cut the four longer pieces of wood 2.5cm (1 in.) longer than the desired loom/square size, and the two shorter pieces of wood 2.5cm (1 in.) shorter than this size (as long as you're using slats with a width of 2.5cm/1 in.). For example, to make a 30cm (12 in.) square loom with wood that is 2.5cm (1 in.) wide, cut four 33cm (13 in.) pieces and two 28cm (11 in.) pieces.

If the slats are 2cm (¾ in.) wide, then the long pieces will be 2cm (¾ in.) longer than the desired loom size, and the short pieces 2cm (¾ in.) shorter.

Use the steps on pages 16–17 to determine nail placement, or otherwise use a photocopier to resize the template opposite by the appropriate percentage.

Opposite: This full-size template will help you to create a 10 x 10cm (4 x 4 in.) loom, like the Zoom Loom or the Weave-It. Don't forget to add the numbers to your new loom – they will help orient you when you are weaving. You may also find it helpful to add arrows, as per the Zoom Loom, noting the directions for threading the loom. The red arrow indicates where to begin weaving a basic square.

Disposable loom

If you are in a rush or don't enjoy woodworking, you can make a quick disposable loom using Styrofoam or foamboard. Buy a 12.5cm (5 in.) square (or cut one from a larger sheet) and place the nails as per the instructions and template on pages 17 and 18. You could use dress-making pins for this. Once the pins are in place, use a craft knife to cut a square hole from the centre, and you'll have a one-time-use loom!

The numbers printed on the corners of the Zoom Loom are referred to in the instructions from page 23 onwards.

19

Setting up the Loom and Weaving Techniques

The twenty-two woven stitches used in this book use two different types of warp thread: three-layer and two-layer. Two more advanced stitches – houndstooth check and Scottish stitch – use variations of these that are explained as part of the instructions for the stitch. You will need about 8.5 metres (9 yards) of yarn to complete one square. For information on the best yarns to use see page 50. The squares in this chapter have been woven using two colours of yarn to make it easier to follow the instructions, but you can make them in one colour – or as many as you like!

Three-layer Warp Thread Setup

The majority of the stitches in this book use the three-layer warp thread setup as a foundation for the weaving. The loom is threaded vertically, horizontally, then vertically again. Finally, you will weave horizontally to finish the square using the 15cm (6 in.) needle. The steps are shown using two colours of yarn to make them easy to follow (yellow for warp, blue for weft). Work on a pale-coloured surface and under a bright light to make it easy for you to see where the threads have been wound.

If you are using a Zoom Loom, always check that the yarn follows the direction of the arrows between the pins. If you are using another loom, consider adding these arrows, as well as the corner numbers, as per the template on page 18. These marks are used in the instructions on the following pages.

Layer one

1 Position the loom so that corner 1 (with the slot that holds the end of the yarn to prevent it becoming tangled) is the bottom left-hand corner.

2 Anchor the thread in the slot, leaving a 4 in. (10cm) tail. Take the yarn to the top corner of the loom (corner 3), in between the vertical and horizontal sets of pins, and around the two pins in the first set of pins.

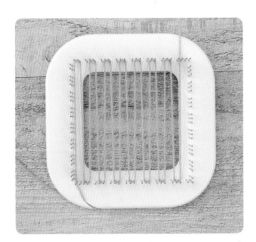

3 Continue threading, taking the yarn up and down the loom, working from left to right, and winding it around the last two pins in each set. At the top right corner (corner 4), wind the yarn around the middle two pins in the set of four.

4 When you reach the bottom right corner of the loom (corner 2), wind the yarn over the corner pin and the one above it. This completes the first warp layer.

Tension

As you weave, use your fingers to tension the yarn. Woollen yarns should sit straight on the loom but not be too tight – you need to retain some of their elasticity to help you to weave through the threads later. Cotton yarns, which are not stretchy, should be left relatively loose.

Wool

Cotton

Layer two

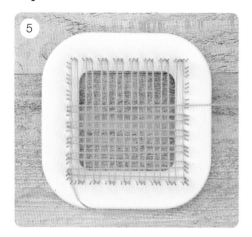

Layer three

Weft threads for basic woven stitch

5 Take the yarn horizontally to the left of the loom and around the last two pins in the first group, making sure it follows the direction of the arrows. Wrap the pins in the same way as the first layer. You may find it easier to turn the loom around 90 degrees and work vertically.

6 When you get to the top left corner of the loom (corner 3), wind the yarn around the first horizontal and vertical pins. This completes the second warp layer.

7 Thread the yarn down the loom and around the two centre pins in the group at the bottom of the loom. Take it back to the top of the loom and around the first two pins of the next group. Continue to weave in this way until you reach the bottom right corner of the loom (corner 2); thread the yarn between the final two groups of pins. This completes the third warp layer.

8 Wind the weaving yarn around the loom six times and then cut it – this is enough yarn to complete a basic woven stitch square.

9 Unwind the thread from around the outside of the loom and thread the 15cm (6 in.) needle supplied with the loom. Starting at the bottom right corner (corner 2), and so working from right to left, weave the needle over the loop outside of the pins and under the next thread between the first two pins. Always go over the loops on the outside of the pins at the beginning of a row – they are not part of the 31 stitch thread count. Continue to weave plain, alternating over and under (abbreviated to W in the stitch patterns) to the end of the row. Work the next row from left to right, taking the yarn around two pins at the end of each row. After completing each row, use the needle to push down the yarn you have just woven to make space for the next row – this is important with thicker yarns where lack of space may make it difficult to weave the last row.

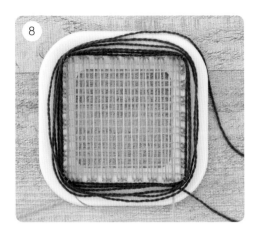

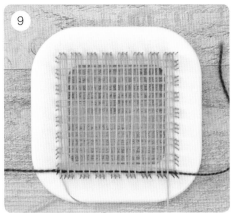

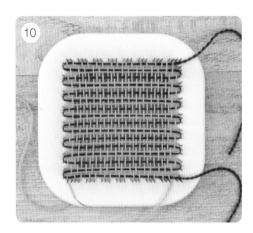

10 When you have threaded yarn between all the pins (16 threads in total) use the needle to neaten the weft threads if necessary. Weave the end of the thread into the square to secure it and trim the end. Repeat to secure the first loose end; you may find it easier to use the 7.5cm (3 in.) needle for this. Carefully remove the square from the loom.

Changing yarn colour

To change yarn colour, simply cut the first colour, leaving a 7.5cm (3 in.) tail, and join in the second colour by tying the ends of the yarns together. This square was woven using the Basic Woven Stitch (see page 26 for the pattern).

Three-layer Warp Thread Stitches

The following stitches are all based on the three-layer warp thread base (see pages 22–25).

Warp is shown in blue, weft in gold for all. The stitches have been abbreviated as follllows:

W weave plain.

O take the yarn over the thread.

U take the yarn under the thread.

Basic Woven Stitch

Row 1: W to end.

Row 2: W to end.

Row 3: W to end.

Row 4: W to end.

Row 5: W to end.

Row 6: W to end.

Row 7: W to end.

Row 8: W to end.

Row 9: W to end.

Row 10: W to end.

Row 11: W to end.

Row 12: W to end.

Row 13: W to end.

Row 14: W to end.

Row 15: W to end.

Row 16: W to end.

Chain Stitch

Row 1: W to end.

Row 2: W2, U3, O1, U3, O1, U3, O1, U3, O1, U3, O1, U3, O1, U3, W2.

Row 3: W to end.

Row 4: W2, U3, O1, U3, O1, U3, O1, U3, O1, U3, O1, U3, O1, U3, W2.

Row 5: W to end.

Row 6: W2, U3, O1, U3, O1, U3, O1, U3, O1, U3, O1, U3, O1, U3, W2.

Row 7: W to end.

Row 8: W2, U3, O1, U3, O1, U3, O1, U3, O1, U3, O1, U3, O1, U3, W2.

Row 9: W to end.

Row 10: W2, U3, O1, U3, O1, U3, O1, U3, O1, U3, O1, U3, O1, U3, W2.

Row 11: W to end.

Row 12: W2, U3, O1, U3, O1, U3, O1, U3, O1, U3, O1, U3, O1, U3, W2.

Row 13: W to end.

Row 14: W2, U3, O1, U3, O1, U3, O1, U3, O1, U3, O1, U3, O1, U3, W2.

Row 15: W to end.

Row 16: W to end.

Clover Stitch

Row 1: W to end.

Row 2: W5, O3, U1, O1, U1, O3, U1, O1, U1, O3, U1, O1, U1, O3, W5.

Row 3: W8, U3, W9, U3, W8.

Row 4: W to end.

Row 5: W5, O3, U1, O1, U1, O3, U1, O1, U1, O3, U1, O1, U1, O3, W5.

Row 6: W8, U3, W9, U3, W8.

Row 7: W to end.

Row 8: W5, O3, U1, O1, U1, O3, U1, O1, U1, O3, U1, O1, U1, O3, W5.

Row 9: W8, U3, W9, U3, W8.

Row 10: W to end.

Row 11: W5, O3, U1, O1, U1, O3, U1, O1, U1, O3, U1, O1, U1, O3, W5.

Row 12: W8, U3, W9, U3, W8.

Row 13: W to end.

Row 14: W5, O3, U1, O1, U1, O3, U1, O1, U1, O3, U1, O1, U1, O3, W5.

Row 15: W8, U3, W9, U3, W8.

Row 16: W to end.

Volume Stitch

Row 1: W to end.

Row 2: U3, O1, U3, O1, U3, O1, U3, O1, U3, O1, U3, O1, U3, O1, U3.

Row 3: U1, O3, U1, O3, U1, O3, U1, O3, U1, O3, U1, O3, U1, O3, W3.

Row 4: U3, O1, U3, O1, U3, O1, U3, O1, U3, O1, U3, O1, U3, O1, U3.

Row 5: U1, O3, U1, O3, U1, O3, U1, O3, U1, O3, U1, O3, U1, O3, W3.

Row 6: U3, O1, U3, O1, U3, O1, U3, O1, U3, O1, U3, O1, U3, O1, U3.

Row 7: U1, O3, U1, O3, U1, O3, U1, O3, U1, O3, U1, O3, U1, O3, W3.

Row 8: U3, O1, U3, O1, U3, O1, U3, O1, U3, O1, U3, O1, U3, O1, U3.

Row 9: U1, O3, U1, O3, U1, O3, U1, O3, U1, O3, U1, O3, U1, O3, W3.

Row 10: U3, O1, U3, O1, U3, O1, U3, O1, U3, O1, U3, O1, U3, O1, U3.

Row 11: U1, O3, U1, O3, U1, O3, U1, O3, U1, O3, U1, O3, U1, O3, W3.

Row 12: U3, O1, U3, O1, U3, O1, U3, O1, U3, O1, U3, O1, U3, O1, U3.

Row 13: U1, O3, U1, O3, U1, O3, U1, O3, U1, O3, U1, O3, U1, O3, W3.

Row 14: U3, O1, U3, O1, U3, O1, U3, O1, U3, O1, U3, O1, U3, O1, U3.

Row 15: U1, O3, U1, O3, U1, O3, U1, O3, U1, O3, U1, O3, U1, O3, W3.

Row 16: W to end.

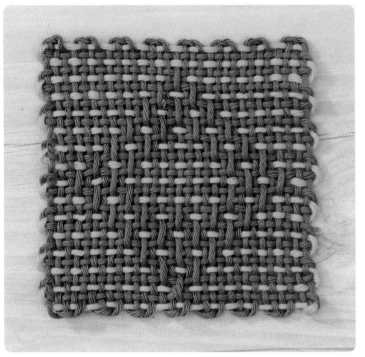

Diamond in Relief Stitch

Row 1: W to end.

Row 2: W14, U3, W14.

Row 3: W12, U3, O1, U3, W12.

Row 4: W10, U3, O1, U3, O1, U3, W10.

Row 5: W8, U3, O1, U3, O1, U3, O1, U3, W8.

Row 6: W6, U3, O1, U3, W5, U3, O1, U3, W6.

Row 7: W4, U3, O1, U3, W9, U3, O1, U3, W4.

Row 8: W2, U3, O1, U3, W13, U3, O1, U3, W2.

Row 9: W4, U3, O1, U3, W9, U3, O1, U3, W4.

Row 10: W6, U3, O1, U3, W5, U3, O1, U3, W6.

Row 11: W8, U3, O1, U3, O1, U3, O1, U3, W8.

Row 12: W10, U3, O1, U3, O1, U3, W10.

Row 13: W12, U3, O1, U3, W12.

Row 14: W14, U3, W14.

Row 15: W to end.

Row 16: W to end.

Outlined X Stitch

Row 1: W to end.

Row 2: W8, U3, W9, U3, W8.

Row 3: W10, U3, W5, U3, W10.

Row 4: U3, W9, U3, O1, U3, W9, U3.

Row 5: W2, U3, W9, U3, W9, U3, W2.

Row 6: W4, U3, W17, U3, W4.

Row 7: W6, U3, W13, U3, W6.

Row 8: W8, U3, W9, U3, W8.

Row 9: W6, U3, W13, U3, W6.

Row 10: W4, U3, W17, U3, W4.

Row 11: W2, U3, W9, U3, W9, U3, W2.

Row 12: U3, W9, U3, O1, U3, W9, U3.

Row 13: W10, U3, W5, U3, W10.

Row 14: W8, U3, W9, U3, W8.

Row 15: W6, U3, W13, U3, W6.

Row 16: W to end.

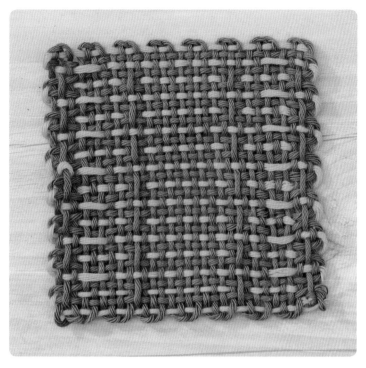

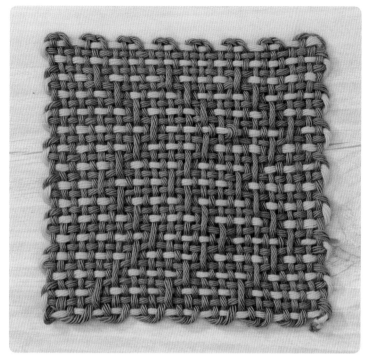

Woven Edge Stitch

Row 1: W to end.

Row 2: U3, W5, U3, W9, U3, W5, U3.

Row 3: W3, O3, W19, O3, W3.

Row 4: U3, W5, U3, W9, U3, W5, U3.

Row 5: W3, O3, W19, O3, W3.

Row 6: U3, W5, U3, W9, U3, W5, U3.

Row 7: W3, O3, W19, O3, W3.

Row 8: U3, W5, U3, W9, U3, W5, U3.

Row 9: W3, O3, W19, O3, W3.

Row 10: U3, W5, U3, W9, U3, W5, U3.

Row 11: W3, O3, W19, O3, W3.

Row 12: U3, W5, U3, W9, U3, W5, U3.

Row 13: W3, O3, W19, O3, W3.

Row 14: U3, W5, U3, W9, U3, W5, U3.

Row 15: W3, O3, W19, O3, W3.

Row 16: W to end.

Triple Zigzag Stitch

Row 1: W to end.

Row 2: W4, U3, W5, U3, W5, U3, W8.

Row 3: W6, U3, W5, U3, W5, U3, W6.

Row 4: W8, U3, W5, U3, W5, U3, W4.

Row 5: W2, U3, W5, U3, W5, U3, W10.

Row 6: W8, U3, W5, U3, W5, U3, W4.

Row 7: W6, U3, W5, U3, W5, U3, W6.

Row 8: W4, U3, W5, U3, W5, U3, W8.

Row 9: W6, U3, W5, U3, W5, U3, W6.

Row 10: W8, U3, W5, U3, W5, U3, W4.

Row 11: W2, U3, W5, U3, W5, U3, W10.

Row 12: W8, U3, W5, U3, W5, U3, W4.

Row 13: W6, U3, W5, U3, W5, U3, W6.

Row 14: W4, U3, W5, U3, W5, U3, W8.

Row 15: W to end.

Row 16: W to end.

W weave plain   **O** take the yarn over the thread   **U** take the yarn under the thread

Double V Stitch

Row 1: W to end.

Row 2: U3, O1, U3, W17, U3, O1, U3.

Row 3: W2, U3, O1, U3, W13, U3, O1, U3, W2.

Row 4: W4, U3, O1, U3, W9, U3, O1, U3, W4.

Row 5: W6, U3, O1, U3, W5, U3, O1, U3, W6.

Row 6: W8, U3, O1, U3, O1, U3, O1, U3, W8.

Row 7: W10, U3, O1, U3, O1, U3, W10.

Row 8: U3, O1, U3, W5, U3, O1, U3, W5, U3, O1, U3.

Row 9: W2, U3, O1, U3, W5, U3, W5, U3, O1, U3, W2.

Row 10: W4, U3, O1, U3, W9, U3, O1, U3, W4.

Row 11: W6, U3, O1, U3, W5, U3, O1, U3, W6.

Row 12: W8, U3, O1, U3, O1, U3, O1, U3, W8.

Row 13: W10, U3, O1, U3, O1, U3, W10.

Row 14: W12, U3, O1, U3, W12.

Row 15: W14, U3, W14.

Row 16: W to end.

Textured Edge Stitch

Row 1: W to end.

Row 2: U3, O1, U3, W17, U3, O1, U3.

Row 3: W2, U3, W21, U3, W2.

Row 4: U3, O1, U3, W17, U3, O1, U3.

Row 5: W2, U3, W21, U3, W2.

Row 6: U3, O1, U3, W17, U3, O1, U3.

Row 7: W2, U3, W21, U3, W2.

Row 8: U3, O1, U3, W17, U3, O1, U3.

Row 9: W2, U3, W21, U3, W2.

Row 10: U3, O1, U3, W17, U3, O1, U3.

Row 11: W2, U3, W21, U3, W2.

Row 12: U3, O1, U3, W17, U3, O1, U3.

Row 13: W2, U3, W21, U3, W2.

Row 14: U3, O1, U3, W17, U3, O1, U3.

Row 15: W2, U3, W21, U3, W2.

Row 16: W to end.

Square in Relief Stitch

Row 1: W to end.

Row 2: W to end.

Row 3: W to end.

Row 4: W6, U3, O1, U3, O1, U3, O1, U3, O1, U3, W6.

Row 5: W8, U3, O1, U3, O1, U3, O1, U3, W8.

Row 6: W6, U3, O1, U3, O1, U3, O1, U3, O1, U3, W6.

Row 7: W8, U3, O1, U3, O1, U3, O1, U3, W8.

Row 8: W6, U3, O1, U3, O1, U3, O1, U3, O1, U3, W6.

Row 9: W8, U3, O1, U3, O1, U3, O1, U3, W8.

Row 10: W6, U3, O1, U3, O1, U3, O1, U3, O1, U3, W6.

Row 11: W8, U3, O1, U3, O1, U3, O1, U3, W8.

Row 12: W6, U3, O1, U3, O1, U3, O1, U3, O1, U3, W6.

Row 13: W8, U3, O1, U3, O1, U3, O1, U3, W8.

Row 14: W to end.

Row 15: W to end.

Row 16: W to end.

Triangle in Relief Stitch

Row 1: W to end.

Row 2: U3, O1, U3, O1, U3, O1, U3, O1, U3, O1, U3, O1, U3, O1, U3.

Row 3: W2, U3, O1, U3, O1, U3, O1, U3, O1, U3, O1, U3, O1, U3, W2.

Row 4: W4, U3, O1, U3, O1, U3, O1, U3, O1, U3, O1, U3, O1, U3.

Row 5: W2, U3, O1, U3, O1, U3, O1, U3, O1, U3, O1, U3, W6.

Row 6: W8, U3, O1, U3, O1, U3, O1, U3, O1, U3, O1, U3.

Row 7: W2, U3, O1, U3, O1, U3, O1, U3, O1, U3, W10.

Row 8: W12, U3, O1, U3, O1, U3, O1, U3, O1, U3.

Row 9: W2, U3, O1, U3, O1, U3, O1, U3, W14.

Row 10: W16, U3, O1, U3, O1, U3, O1, U3.

Row 11: W2, U3, O1, U3, O1, U3, W18.

Row 12: W20, U3, O1, U3, O1, U3.

Row 13: W2, U3, O1, U3, W22.

Row 14: W24, U3, O1, U3.

Row 15: W2, U3, W26.

Row 16: W to end.

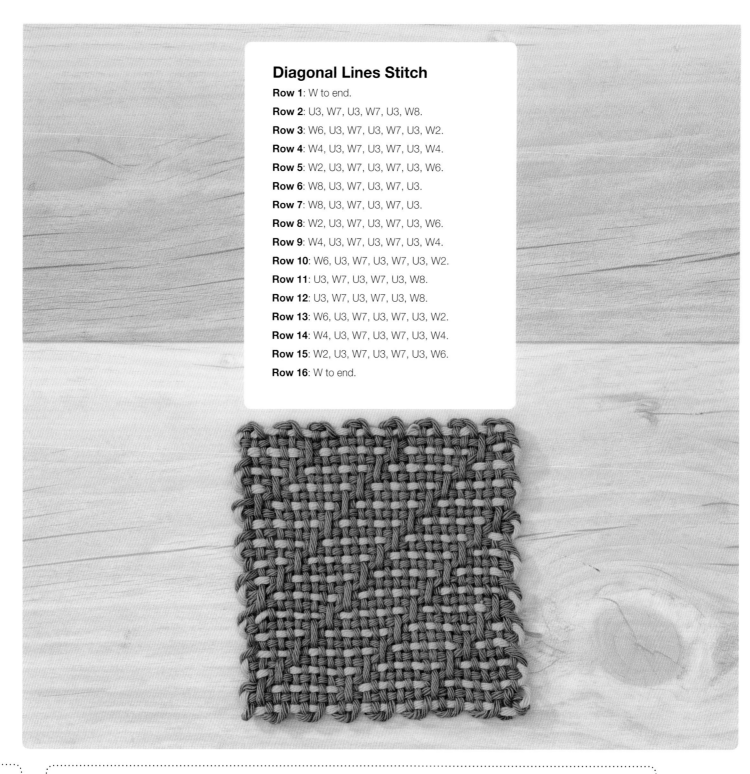

Diagonal Lines Stitch

Row 1: W to end.

Row 2: U3, W7, U3, W7, U3, W8.

Row 3: W6, U3, W7, U3, W7, U3, W2.

Row 4: W4, U3, W7, U3, W7, U3, W4.

Row 5: W2, U3, W7, U3, W7, U3, W6.

Row 6: W8, U3, W7, U3, W7, U3.

Row 7: W8, U3, W7, U3, W7, U3.

Row 8: W2, U3, W7, U3, W7, U3, W6.

Row 9: W4, U3, W7, U3, W7, U3, W4.

Row 10: W6, U3, W7, U3, W7, U3, W2.

Row 11: U3, W7, U3, W7, U3, W8.

Row 12: U3, W7, U3, W7, U3, W8.

Row 13: W6, U3, W7, U3, W7, U3, W2.

Row 14: W4, U3, W7, U3, W7, U3, W4.

Row 15: W2, U3, W7, U3, W7, U3, W6.

Row 16: W to end.

W weave plain   **O** take the yarn over the thread   **U** take the yarn under the thread

Honeycomb Stitch

Row 1: W to end.

Row 2: W2, U3, O1, U3, O1, U3, O1, U3, O1, U3, O1,U3, O1, U3, W2.

Row 3: U3, O1, U3, O1, U3, O1, U3, O1, U3, O1, U3, O1, U3, O1, U2, O1.

Row 4: W2, U3, O1, U3, O1, U3, O1, U3, O1, U3, O1,U3, O1, U3, W2.

Row 5: U3, O1, U3, O1, U3, O1, U3, O1, U3, O1, U3, O1, U3, O1, U2, O1.

Row 6: W2, U3, O1, U3, O1, U3, O1, U3, O1, U3, O1,U3, O1, U3, W2.

Row 7: U3, O1, U3, O1, U3, O1, U3, O1, U3, O1, U3, O1, U3, O1, U2, O1.

Row 8: W2, U3, O1, U3, O1, U3, O1, U3, O1, U3, O1,U3, O1, U3, W2.

Row 9: U3, O1, U3, O1, U3, O1, U3, O1, U3, O1, U3, O1, U3, O1, U2, O1.

Row 10: W2, U3, O1, U3, O1, U3, O1, U3, O1, U3, O1,U3, O1, U3, W2.

Row 11: U3, O1, U3, O1, U3, O1, U3, O1, U3, O1, U3, O1, U3, O1, U2, O1.

Row 12: W2, U3, O1, U3, O1, U3, O1, U3, O1, U3, O1,U3, O1, U3, W2.

Row 13: U3, O1, U3, O1, U3, O1, U3, O1, U3, O1, U3, O1, U3, O1, U2, O1.

Row 14: W2, U3, O1, U3, O1, U3, O1, U3, O1, U3, O1,U3, O1, U3, W2.

Row 15: U3, O1, U3, O1, U3, O1, U3, O1, U3, O1, U3, O1, U3, O1, U2, O1.

Row 16: W to end.

Scottish Stitch

This stitch is started in the same way as the three-layer warp thread (see page 22), and woven as the basic woven stitch (see page 26). Here blue is used for colour 1 and yellow for colour 2.

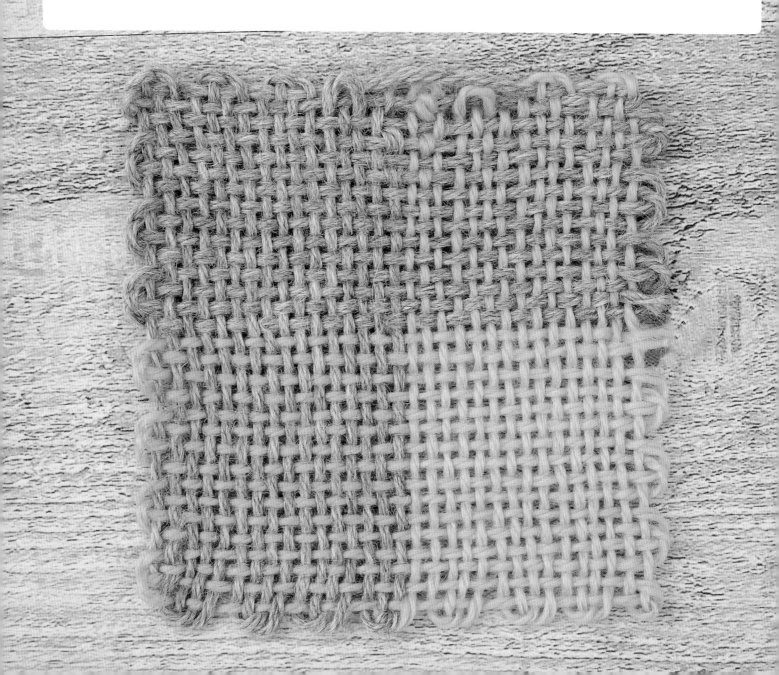

Layer one

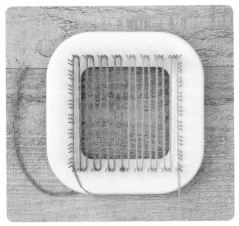

1 After threading eight rows with colour 1, cut the yarn and join in colour 2 by tying the ends of the yarns together. Use colour 2 to complete layer one.

Layer two

2 Join colour 1 in again and work layer two in the same way as the three-layer warp thread, using the two colours in the same order and changing again after thread 8.

Layer three

3 Work layer three in the same way as Step 1.

Weaving

4 Wind the yarn (colour 2) around the loom three times and cut it. Unwind and use to thread the 15cm (6 in.) needle. Start weaving in the bottom right corner (corner 2). Weave plain.

5 After row 8, change to colour 1, wrap it around the loom three times to measure, then cut. Weave to the end. The square is now complete.

6 Weave all the ends into the woven fabric within a square of the matching colour to disguise them.

Two-layer Warp Thread Setup

The two-layer warp thread setup is a useful alternative to the three-layer version shown on pages 22–25. The loom is threaded vertically in two layers of parallel threads before it is woven horizontally. Again, two colours of yarn have been used to show the steps clearly (orange for warp, yellow for weft). Once you have wound the loom, use the needle to weave one of the stitches shown on pages 40–45.

Layer one

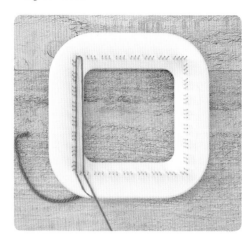

1 Position the loom as per the three-layer warp. Take the yarn vertically to the top of the loom and around the two pins in the first group, following the direction of the arrows between the pins.

2 Continue weaving, taking the yarn up and down the loom, working from left to right, and around the last two pins in each group of pins. At corner 4, wind the yarn around the middle two pins in the set of four.

3 When you reach the bottom right corner of the loom (corner 2), take the yarn around the second pin on the bottom of the loom and start to take the yarn back to the top. This completes the first warp layer.

Layer two

4 Thread the yarn vertically, working from right to left and taking it around the last two pins in each group. To complete this layer, thread the yarn between the last two pins in the top left corner (corner 3).

5 Turn the loom 180 degrees and wind the yarn around the loom eight times, then cut. Thread the 15cm (6 in.) needle and wind the yarn around the pin in the bottom right corner (of the horizontal row of pins), now corner 3.

Begin weaving one of the stitches on pages 40–45. When you reach corner 4, wind the yarn round the pin in the bottom left corner, then return to corner 3, looping around the second pin in the first group of two. For the remaining rows, omit the middle pin of each group and finish between the last two pins at the top of the left side (corner 2); this will give you 31 rows in total.

Two-layer Warp Thread Stitches

The following stitches are all based on the two-layer warp thread base. Warp is shown in purple, weft in green for all. There are no loops in a two-layer warp setup, so begin row 1 by weaving under the first thread, then carry on weaving plain as indicated by the pattern direction (U) W.

Arrow Stitch

Row 1: (U) W31 (reach the pin in the bottom corner).

Row 2: O2, U2 (repeat to end).

Row 3: O2, U2 (repeat to end).

Row 4: O1, U1, O2, U2 (repeat O2, U2 to end).

Row 5: U2, O2 (repeat to end).

Row 6: U1, O1, U2, O2 (repeat U2, O2 to end).

Row 7: O2, U2 (repeat to end).

Row 8: O1, U1, O2, U2 (repeat O2, U2 to end).

Row 9: U2, O2 (repeat to end).

Row 10: U1, O1, U2, O2 (repeat U2, O2 to end).

Row 11: O2, U2 (repeat to end).

Row 12: O1, U1, O2, U2 (repeat O2, U2 to end).

Row 13: U2, O2 (repeat to end).

Row 14: U1, O1, U2, O2 (repeat U2, O2 to end).

Row 15: O2, U2 (repeat to end).

Row 16: O1, U1, O2, U2 (repeat O2, U2 to end).

Row 17: U1, O1, U2, O2 (repeat U2, O2 to end).

Row 18: O2, U2 (repeat to end).

Row 19: O1, U1, O2, U2 (repeat O2, U2 to end).

Row 20: U2, O2 (repeat to end).

Row 21: U1, O1, U2, O2 (repeat U2, O2 to end).

Row 22: O2, U2 (repeat to end).

Row 23: O1, U1, O2, U2 (repeat O2, U2 to end).

Row 24: U2, O2 (repeat to end).

Row 25: U1, O1, U2, O2 (repeat U2, O2 to end).

Row 26: O2, U2 (repeat to end).

Row 27: O1, U1, O2, U2 (repeat O2, U2 to end).

Row 28: U2, O2 (repeat to end).

Row 29: U1, O1, U2, O2 (repeat U2, O2 to end).

Row 30: O2, U2 (repeat to end).

Row 31: O2, U1, W28.

Diamond Stitch

Row 1: U1, O1, U1, O2, U2, O2, U2, O2, U2, O1, U2, O2, U2, O2, U2, O2, U2, O1.

Row 2: U2, O2, U2, O2, U2, O2, U2, O3, U2, O2, U2, O2, U2, O2, U1, O1.

Row 3: U1, O2, U2, O2, U2, O2, U2, O2, U1, O2, U2, O2, U2, O2, U2, O3.

Row 4: U1, O1, U2, O2, U2, O2, U2, O2, U3, O2, U2, O2, U2, O2, U2, O1, U1.

Row 5: O1, U2, O2, U2, O2, U2, O2, U2, O1, U2, O2, U2, O2, U2, O2, U2, O1.

Row 6: U2, O2, U2, O2, U2, O2, U2, O3, U2, O2, U2, O2, U2, O2, U1, O1.

Row 7: U1, O2, U2, O2, U2, O2, U2, O2, U1, O2, U2, O2, U2, O2, U2, O2, U1.

Row 8: O2, U2, O2, U2, O2, U2, O2, U3, O2, U2, O2, U2, O2, U2, O1, U1.

Row 9: O1, U2, O2, U2, O2, U2, O2, U2, O1, U2, O2, U2, O2, U2, O2, U2, O1.

Row 10: U2, O2, U2, O2, U2, O2, U2, O3, U2, O2, U2, O2, U2, O2, U1, O1.

Row 11: U1, O2, U2, O2, U2, O2, U2, O2, U1, O2, U2, O2, U2, O2, U2, O2, U1.

Row 12: O2, U2, O2, U2, O2, U2, O2, U3, O2, U2, O2, U2, O2, U2, O1, U1.

Row 13: O1, U2, O2, U2, O2, U2, O2, U2, O1, U2, O2, U2, O2, U2, O2, U2, O1.

Row 14: U2, O2, U2, O2, U2, O2, U2, O3, U2, O2, U2, O2, U2, O2, U1, O1.

Row 15: U1, O2, U2, O2, U2, O2, U2, O2, U1, O2, U2, O2, U2, O2, U2, O2, U1.

Row 16: O2, U2, O2, U2, O2, U2, O2, U3, O2, U2, O2, U2, O2, U2, O1, U1.

Row 17: O1, U2, O2, U2, O2, U2, O2, U2, O1, U2, O2, U2, O2, U2, O2, U2, O1.

Row 18: U1, O1, U2, O2, U2, O2, U2, O2, U3, O2, U2, O2, U2, O2, U2, O2.

Row 19: U1, O2, U2, O2, U2, O2, U2, O2, U1, O2, U2, O2, U2, O2, U2, O2, U1.

Row 20: O1, U1, O2, U2, O2, U2, O2, U2, O3, U2, O2, U2, O2, U2, O2, U2.

Row 21: O1, U2, O2, U2, O2, U2, O2, U2, O1, U2, O2, U2, O2, U2, O2, U1, O1, U1.

Row 22: O2, U2, O2, U2, O2, U2, O2, U3, O2, U2, O2, U2, O2, U2, O2.

Row 23: U1, O2, U2, O2, U2, O2, U2, O2, U1, O2, U2, O2, U2, O2, U2, O2, U1.

Row 24: O1, U1, O2, U2, O2, U2, O2, U2, O3, U2, O2, U2, O2, U2, O2, U2.

Row 25: O1, U2, O2, U2, O2, U2, O2, U2, O1, U2, O2, U2, O2, U2, O2, U2, O1.

Row 26: U1, O1, U2, O2, U2, O2, U2, O2, U3, O2, U2, O2, U2, O2, U2, O2.

Row 27: U1, O2, U2, O2, U2, O2, U2, O2, U1, O2, U2, O2, U2, O2, U2, O2, U1.

Row 28: O1, U1, O2, U2, O2, U2, O2, U2, O3, U2, O2, U2, O2, U2, O2, U2.

Row 29: O1, U2, O2, U2, O2, U2, O2, U2, O1, U2, O2, U2, O2, U2, O2, U2, O1.

Row 30: U1, O1, U2, O2, U2, O2, U2, O2, U3, O2, U2, O2, U2, O2, U2, O1, U1.

Row 31: O1, U1, O1, U2, O2, U2, O2, U2, O2, U1, O2, U2, O2, U2, O2, U2, O2, U1.

X Stitch

Row 1: (U) W29, O2.

Row 2: U1, O2, U2, O2, W17, O2, U2, O2, U1.

Row 3: O1, U1, O2, U2, O2, W15, O2, U2, O2, U2.

Row 4: O1, U2, O2, U2, O2, W13, O2, U2, O2, U3.

Row 5: O2, U2, O2, U2, O2, W11, O2, U2, O2, U2, O2.

Row 6: U1, O2, U2, O2, U2, O2, W9, O2, U2, O2, U2, O2, U1.

Row 7: O1, U1, O2, U2, O2, U2, O2, W7, O2, U2, O2, U2, O2, U2.

Row 8: O1, U2, O2, U2, O2, U2, O2, W5, O2, U2, O2, U2, O2, U2, O1.

Row 9: U1, O1, U2, O2, U2, O2, U2, O2, W3, O2, U2, O2, U2, O2, O2.

Row 10: U1, O2, U2, O2, U2, O2, U2, O2, U1, O2, U2, O2, U2, O2, U2, O2, U1.

Row 11: O1, U1, O2, U2, O2, U2, O2, U2, O3, U2, O2, U2, O2, U2, O2, U2.

Row 12: O1, U2, O2, U2, O2, U2, O2, U2, O1, U2, O2, U2, O2, U2, O2, U2, O1.

Row 13: U1, O1, U2, O2, U2, O2, U2, O2, U3, O2, U2, O2, U2, O2, U2, O1, U1.

Row 14: O1, U1, O1, U2, O2, U2, O2, U2, O2, U1, O2, U2, O2, U2, O2, U2, O1, U1, O1.

Row 15: (U) W4, U2, O2, U2, O2, U2, O3, U2, O2, U2, O2, U2, W4.

Row 16: (O) W5, U2, O2, U2, O2, U2, O1, U2, O2, U2, O2, U2, W5.

Row 17: (U) W4, U2, O2, U2, O2, U2, O3, U2, O2, U2, O2, U2, W4.

Row 18: O1, U1, O1, U2, O2, U2, O2, U2, O2, U1, O2, U2, O2, U2, O2, U2, O1, U1, O1.

Row 19: U1, O1, U2, O2, U2, O2, U2, O2, U3, O2, U2, O2, U2, O2, U2, O1, U1.

Row 20: O1, U2, O2, U2, O2, U2, O2, U2, O1, U2, O2, U2, O2, U2, O2, U2, O1.

Row 21: U2, O2, U2, O2, U2, O2, U2, O3, U2, O2, U2, O2, U2 O2, U1, O1.

Row 22: U1, O2, U2, O2, U2, O2, U2, O2, U1, O2, U2, O2, U2 O2, U2, O2, U1.

Row 23: O2, U2, O2, U2, O2, U2, O2, W3, O2, U2, O2, U2, O2, U2, O1, U1.

Row 24: O1, U2, O2, U2, O2, U2, O2, W5, O2, U2, O2, U2, O2 U2, O1.

Row 25: U2, O2, U2, O2, U2, O2, W6, U1, O2, U2, O2, U2, O2, U1, O1.

Row 26: U1, O2, U2, O2, U2, O2, W9, O2, U2, O2, U2, O2, U1.

Row 27: O2, U2, O2, U2, O2, W11, O2, U2, O2, U2, O1, U1.

Row 28: O1, U2, O2, U2, O2, W13, O2, U2, O2, U2, O1.

Row 29: U2, O2, U2, O2, W15, O2, U2, O2, U1, O1.

Row 30: U1, O2, U2, O2, W17, O2, U2, O2, U1.

Row 31: O2, W29.

Multiple Diamonds Stitch

Row 1: (U) W 29, O2.

Row 2: U1, O1, U3, O2, U2, O1, U2, O2, U3, O2, U2, O1, U2, O2, U3, O1, U1.

Row 3: O1, U2, O1, U2, O2, U3, O2, U2, O1, U2, O2, U3, O2, U2, O1, U2, O1.

Row 4: U2, O3, U2, O2, U1, O2, U2, O3, U2, O2, U1, O2, U2, O3, U1, O1.

Row 5: U1, O2, U1, O2, U2, O3, U2, O2, U1, O2, U2, O3, U2, O2, U1, O2, U1.

Row 6: O2, U3, O2, U2, O1, U2, O2, U3, O2, U2, O1, U2, O2, U3, O2.

Row 7: U1, O2, U1, O2, U2, O3, U2, O2, U1, O2, U2, O3, U2, O2, U1, O2, U1.

Row 8: O1, U1, O3, U2, O2, U1, O2, U2, O3, U2, O2, U1, O2, U2, O3, U1, O1.

Row 9: O1, U2, O1, U2, O2, U3, O2, U2, O1, U2, O2, U3, O2, U2, O1, U2, O1.

Row 10: U1, O1, U3, O2, U2, O1, U2, O2, U3, O2, U2, O1, U2, O2, U3, O2.

Row 11: U1, O2, U1, O2, U2, O3, U2, O2, U1, O2, U2, O3, U2, O2, U1, O2, U1.

Row 12: O1, U1, O3, U2, O2, U1, O2, U2, O3, U2, O2, U1, O2, U2, O3, U1, O1.

Row 13: U1, O2, U1, O2, U2, O3, U2, O2, U1, O2, U2, O3, U2, O2, U1, O2, U1.

Row 14: O2, U3, O2, U2, O1, U2, O2, U3, O2, U2, O1, U2, O2, U3, O1, U1.

Row 15: O1, U2, O1, U2, O2, U3, O2, U2, O1, U2, O2, U3, O2, U2, O1, U2, O1.

Row 16: U2, O3, U2, O2, U1, O2, U2, O3, U2, O2, U1, O2, U2, O3, U1, O1.

Row 17: U1, O2, U1, O2, U2, O3, U2, O2, U1, O2, U2, O3, U2, O2, U1, O2, U1.

Row 18: O2, U3, O2, U2, O1, U2, O2, U3, O2, U2, O1, U2, O2, U3, O2.

Row 19: U1, O2, U1, O2, U2, O3, U2, O2, U1, O2, U2, O3, U2, O2, U1, O2, U1.

Row 20: O1, U1, O3, U2, O2, U1, O2, U2, O3, U2, O2, U1, O2, U2, O3, U2.

Row 21: O1, U2, O1, U2, O2, U3, O2, U2, O1, U2, O2, U3, O2, U2, O1, U2, O1.

Row 22: U1, O1, U3, O2, U2, O1, U2, O2, U3, O2, U2, O1, U2, O2, U3, O2.

Row 23: U1, O2, U1, O2, U2, O3, U2, O2, U1, O2, U2, O3, U2, O2, U1, O2, U1.

Row 24: O1, U1, O3, U2, O2, U1, O2, U2, O3, U2, O2, U1, O2, U2, O3, U1, O1.

Row 25: U1, O2, U1, O2, U2, O3, U2, O2, U1, O2, U2, O3, U2, O2, U1, O2, U1.

Row 26: O2, U3, O2, U2, O1, U2, O2, U3, O2, U2, O1, U2, O2, U3, O1, U1.

Row 27: O1, U2, O1, U2, O2, U3, O2, U2, O1, U2, O2, U3, O2, U2, O1, U2, O1.

Row 28: U2, O3, U2, O2, U1, O2, U2, O3, U2, O2, U1, O2, U2, O3, U1, O1.

Row 29: U1, O2, U1, O2, U2, O3, U2, O2, U1, O2, U2, O3, U2, O2, U1, O2, U1.

Row 30: O2, U3, O2, U2, O1, U2, O2, U3, O2, U2, O1, U2, O2, U3, O2.

Row 31: (U) W 31.

Diagonal Stitch

Row 1: (U) W31 (until you reach the pin in the corner).

Row 2: O2, U2 (repeat to end).

Row 3: O2, U2 (repeat to end).

Row 4: O1, U1, O2, U2 (repeat O2, U2 to end).

Row 5: U2, O2 (repeat to end).

Row 6: U1, O1, U2, O2 (repeat U2, O2 to end).

Row 7: O2, U2 (repeat to end).

Row 8: O1, U1, O2, U2 (repeat O2, U2 to end).

Row 9: U2, O2 (repeat to end).

Row 10: U1, O1, U2, O2 (repeat U2, O2 to end).

Row 11: O2, U2 (repeat to end).

Row 12: O1, U1, O2, U2 (repeat O2, U2 to end).

Row 13: U2, O2 (repeat to end).

Row 14: U1, O1, U2, O2 (repeat U2, O2 to end).

Row 15: O2, U2 (repeat to end).

Row 16: O1, U1, O2, U2 (repeat O2, U2 to end).

Row 17: U2, O2 (repeat to end).

Row 18: U1, O1, U2, O2 (repeat U2, O2 to end).

Row 19: O2, U2 (repeat to end).

Row 20: O1, U1, O2, U2 (repeat O2, U2 to end).

Row 21: U2, O2 (repeat to end).

Row 22: U1, O1, U2, O2 (repeat U2, O2 to end).

Row 23: O2, U2 (repeat to end).

Row 24: O1, U1, O2, U2 (repeat O2, U2 to end).

Row 25: U2, O2 (repeat to end).

Row 26: U1, O1, U2, O2 (repeat U2, O2 to end).

Row 27: O2, U2 (repeat to end).

Row 28: O1, U1, O2, U2 (repeat O2, U2 to end).

Row 29: U2, O2 (repeat to end).

Row 30: U1, O1, U2, O2 (repeat U2, O2 to end).

Row 31: O2, U2, O2 (repeat U2, O2 to end).

Basketweave Stitch

Row 1: (U) W31.

Row 2: (O) W31.

Row 3: U1, O1, U3, O3, U3, O3, U3, O3, U3, O3, U3, O1, U1.

Row 4: O1, U4, O3, U3, O3, U3, O3, U3, O3, U4, O1.

Row 5: U1, O1, U3, O3, U3, O3, U3, O3, U3, O3, U3, O1, U1.

Row 6: O1, U1, O3, U3, O3, U3, O3, U3, O3, U3, O3, U1, O1.

Row 7: U1, O4, U3, O3, U3, O3, U3, O3, U3, O4, U1.

Row 8: O1, U1, O3, U3, O3, U3, O3, U3, O3, U3, O3, U1, O1.

Row 9: U1, O1, U3, O3, U3, O3, U3, O3, U3, O3, U3, O1, U1.

Row 10: O1, U4, O3, U3, O3, U3, O3, U3, O3, U4, O1.

Row 11: U1, O1, U3, O3, U3, O3, U3, O3, U3, O3, U3, O1, U1.

Row 12: O1, U1, O3, U3, O3, U3, O3, U3, O3, U3, O3, U1, O1.

Row 13: U1, O4, U3, O3, U3, O3, U3, O3, U3, O4, U1.

Row 14: O1, U1, O3, U3, O3, U3, O3, U3, O3, U3, O3, U1, O1.

Row 15: U1, O1, U3, O3, U3, O3, U3, O3, U3, O3, U3, O1, U1.

Row 16: O1, U4, O3, U3, O3, U3, O3, U3, O3, U4, O1.

Row 17: U1, O1, U3, O3, U3, O3, U3, O3, U3, O3, U3, O1, U1.

Row 18: O1, U1, O3, U3, O3, U3, O3, U3, O3, U3, O3, U1, O1.

Row 19: U1, O4, U3, O3, U3, O3, U3, O3, U3, O4, U1.

Row 20: O1, U1, O3, U3, O3, U3, O3, U3, O3, U3, O3, U1, O1.

Row 21: U1, O1, U3, O3, U3, O3, U3, O3, U3, O3, U3, O1, U1.

Row 22: O1, U4, O3, U3, O3, U3, O3, U3, O3, U4, O1.

Row 23: U1, O1, U3, O3, U3, O3, U3, O3, U3, O3, U3, O1, U1.

Row 24: O1, U1, O3, U3, O3, U3, O3, U3, O3, U3, O3, U1.

Row 25: U1, O4, U3, O3, U3, O3, U3, O3, U3, O4, U1.

Row 26: O1, U1, O3, U3, O3, U3, O3, U3, O3, U3, O3, U1, O1.

Row 27: U1, O1, U3, O3, U3, O3, U3, O3, U3, O3, U3, O1, U1.

Row 28: O1, U4, O3, U3, O3, U3, O3, U3, O3, U4, O1.

Row 29: U1, O1, U3, O3, U3, O3, U3, O3, U3, O3, U3, O1, U1.

Row 30: (O) W31.

Row 31: (U) W31.

Houndstooth Check Stitch

The warp thread for this stitch is worked in a different way. Pay attention when winding and weaving as there are a lot of threads to work with.

Layer one

1 Start by anchoring the yarn at corner 1 and taking it up the loom and around the first pin at the top of the loom. Take it back to the bottom of the loom and wind it around the first group of three pins. Continue to thread the yarn in this way, passing around one pin at the top and three at the bottom. When you reach the bottom right corner, (corner 2), tie the yarn around the second pin from the base but do not cut it.

Layer two

2 Begin the second layer in the same corner as the first, using a second colour of yarn and starting after the second pin on the bottom row. Take the yarn around the second pin at the top of the loom. When the yarn returns to the bottom of the loom, wind it around the last pin of the left-hand group and the first pin of the right-hand group. At the top of the loom take the yarn around the last pin in every group of three. Continue

Weaving

in this way until you reach the bottom right corner, (corner 2). Tie the yarn as in Step 1 and do not cut it.

3 Wind the second yarn around the loom five times, unwind and cut. Thread the 15cm (6 in.) needle with this yarn and weave under one thread and over the next to the end of the row.

4 Weave the yarn as described in Step 3, taking it around the same pin pattern as layer one, (Step 1), but working horizontally rather than vertically until you reach the top right corner, (corner 4). Leave the thread loose.

5 Wind the first yarn around the loom five times, unwind and cut. Thread the 15cm (6 in.) needle with this yarn and start in the same place as the previous layer. Use the needle to weave the yarn as described in Step 3, taking it around the same pin pattern

as layer two (Step 2) but working horizontally rather than vertically until you reach the bottom right corner, (corner 4). Weave in the ends using a needle as before.

Finishing and Joining the Squares

Place two squares together, matching the corners and checking the position of any pattern to make sure they are correctly aligned on the finished item. Use a matching yarn and weave in the ends to ensure your seams are secure.

Whipstitch

This stitch is quick to work and ideal for joining squares together. Place the right sides of the fabric squares together, insert the needle from the front to the back of the two squares. Bring the needle back to the front and repeat until the seam is finished.

Lace Stitch

Place two squares together with right sides facing you. Take the needle through the first loop of the right square, then the second loop of the left square. Continue, working from right to left to the end. Do not pull the thread too tight or the seam may pucker.

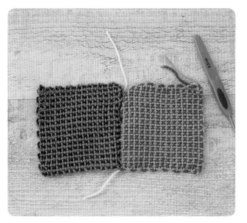

Blocking

Blocking the woven squares creates a neat finish and makes joining them easier. There are two methods: cold-water and steam.

For cold-water blocking, place a square on a folded towel with the right side facing up and pin to the correct size. Spray with cold water to dampen it, but do not over-saturate it. Let dry completely before removing the pins.

For steam blocking, lay a square right-side down on a lightly dampened towel and pin to the correct size. Cover with another lightly dampened towel and hold a steam iron about 5cm (2 in.) above the towels. Steam the square through the towels. Let cool and dry completely before removing the pins.

You can pin two squares together to make sure they are the same size and shape.

Kitchener Stitch

The Kitchener Stitch seam is an invisible seam and it is used to sew fabrics together. Unlike many seams, it has no bulk, and it is used mostly in garment construction. Place the woven pieces on a flat surface with the right sides facing up. Take time to make sure the rows of threads are aligned. Thread the needle through the bottom right loop, cross over to the corresponding left loop, and at the same time draw the yarn through the fabric. Continue working back and forth through the woven threads. Gently tighten the seam while you work, being careful not to make it too tight.

Single Crochet

This stitch creates a decorative border as well as joining squares together. If you do not wish to see the join on the right side, work the seam on the reverse of the pattern squares.

1 Insert a crochet hook through the edge of both squares.
2 Bring the yarn over the hook and pull up a loop. You will have two loops on the hook.
3 Yarn over the hook again and draw it through both loops on the hook to complete the stitch. Insert the hook to start the next stitch and complete Steps 2 and 3. Repeat to the end and secure the yarn ends.

Choosing Yarns

The patterns in this book suggest yarns you can use to weave pin loom squares. However, you can choose other yarns if you wish. If you are new to weaving, try a DK (double knitting) or sportweight yarn. It is elastic and not too thick, making it easy to wind around the pins and weave through them. Once you have become confident, try a cotton yarn – they are easy to work with but less elastic so you will need to adjust your tension (see page 23). Other yarns with little stretch include chenille and linen.

When choosing yarns, think about what the item will be used for. Will it have to withstand a lot of wear? Will it require frequent washing? If so, a machine-washable light or heavy worsted yarn may be ideal.

If you want to create interesting woven fabrics, try combining different yarns, perhaps a 4-ply wool with a mohair or angora yarn for added texture. It is best to use fragile yarns for the warp threads and then something more robust – but fine – for weft weaving. These are less likely to snag or become tangled as they are pulled backwards and forwards through the threads.

Add 'yarns' such as ribbons, raffia, string, strips of fabric and novelty yarns to bring added interest to your woven fabrics.

Yarns are made from three different types of fibre: animal, plant and synthetic (man-made). Some yarns use just one, others combine them to make durable, easy-to-care-for yarns. Each type will bring different qualities to a fabric that need to be considered when selecting yarns for a project.

The most common animal fibre is wool, which is made from the fleece of many different sheep breeds (some yarns even say which breed). It is warm, insulating and elastic; the fibres breathe well and are absorbent. Superwash wool has been treated to allow it to be washed in a machine without shrinking. Other animal fibres include mohair, cashmere, angora, alpaca and silk.

Plant fibres such as cotton, linen and bamboo tend to be lightweight and are ideal for light, summer clothing. Like animal fibres, they breathe well. Mercerised cottons, such as crochet threads, have been specially treated to produce a strong yarn that has a sheen.

Man-made fibres include acrylic, nylon, polyester and rayon. As they can be machine washed and dried they are ideal for baby clothes and pet accessories that require frequent washing. They are also durable and tend to be inexpensive.

Choosing Colours

Selecting the colours for a set of woven squares can be a very satisfying part of the weaving process. If you already have clear ideas about the colour scheme, you can experiment by rolling different colours of wool in your hand and choosing the best proportions and tones.

But if you're unsure of how to combine colours, a quick dip into colour theory may help.

The primary colours – red, yellow and blue – are mixed in different proportions to create all other colours. Mixing the colours that are adjacent to each other on the colour wheel creates the secondary colours: green, orange and purple. Combining a primary and secondary colour make the tertiary colours: yellow-orange, red-orange, red-purple, blue-purple, blue-green and yellow-green.

When choosing the colours for a project, look for harmonious combinations. There are many ways to combine these, but the basic ones follow these guidelines. A monochromatic scheme uses variations of a single colour. I used this sort of scheme for squares including D1, E1, E2, O2, P4 and T1 on pages 63, 66, 86, 87 and 95.

Three colours that sit next to each other on the colour wheel are called analogous colours; one of them will tend to dominate the other two. For examples see squares G3 and H3 on pages 70 and 71.

Complementary colours are two shades that sit opposite each other on the colour wheel. The result is the maximum contrast between two shades. Look at square R4 on page 91 for a good example of this.

Contrasting colours often take their inspiration from nature – for example, a bright pink flower with deep green leaves. These combinations do not follow any rules, but create a harmonious fabric. I used them for squares C2, Q3, U2 and V3 on pages 62, 90, 98 and 99.

When choosing colours you should also think about the saturation – how vivid or intense a colour is – and how different levels of saturation look together.

Most of all though, think about what colours you like, and create squares and projects that will make you happy.

Gallery of Squares

The colourful squares on the following pages show the effect of using different colour combinations to weave the stitches from the previous chapter (see pages 22–47). I have used natural fibres in different weights of yarn, and for each example listed the warp and weft colours. Each square uses two or three colours from a group of four I have chosen. There is a total of eleven colour combinations, making 88 squares – plus 12 additional squares woven with novelty yarns to show off the versatility of the standard weave.

Moss and Heathers

These contrasting warm and cool colours
work together because they are all at
the same saturation. The thickness of
the Cascade Yarns 128 Superwash yarn
suits the loom; it won't become loose
or tight and is easy to weave, making it
great for beginners.

Yarns Used

**Cascade Yarns 128 Superwash Aran in
1944 Blue Heather, 841 Moss, 1919
Turtle, 1983 Peacock, 1982 Harvest
Orange
Fibre: 100% superwash merino wool;
100g (3½ oz); 117m (128 yds)
Weight: Chunky**

Textured Edge Stitch

The appearance of the Textured Edge Stitch is maintained when woven with two or three contrasting colours, making it a versatile weave to use. The technique used to make this square is shown on page 32.

A1

Three warp layers in
1944 Blue Heather
Weave in 1919 Turtle

Warp

Weave

A2

Three warp layers in
1983 Peacock
Weave in 1982
Harvest Orange

Warp

Weave

A3

Two warp layers in
1944 Blue Heather
Third warp layer in
841 Moss
Weave in 1919 Turtle

Warp

Weave

A4

Two warp layers in
1983 Peacock
Third warp layer in
1982 Harvest Orange
Weave in 1919 Turtle

Warp

Weave

Diagonal Stitch

The Diagonal Stitch works well with two colours but you start to lose the diagonal effect when you use three colours and it starts to look like a different stitch. The technique used to make this square is shown on page 44.

B1

Two warp layers in
1944 Blue Heather
Weave in 841 Moss

Warp

Weave

B2

Two warp layers in
1983 Peacock
Weave in 1982
Harvest Orange

Warp

Weave

B3

First warp layer in
1944 Blue Heather
Second warp layer in
841 Moss
Weave in 1919 Turtle

Warp

Weave

B4

First warp layer in
1983 Peacock
Second warp layer in
1982 Harvest Orange
Weave in 1919 Turtle

Warp

Weave

Illuminated Contrasts

These colours create interesting contrasts. In this combination, I wanted to play with the different contrasts. The illuminated yellow and purple work well with the darker, less saturated, blue and turquoise. Cascade Yarns 220 Superwash Sport yarn creates a soft and delicate fabric, especially when using the two-layer warp thread (see pages 38–39).

Yarns Used

Cascade Yarns 220 Superwash Sport in 8398 Navy, 9420 Como Blue, 7808 Purple Hyacinth, 7827 Goldenrod

Fibre: 100% Peruvian Highland wool; 50g (1½ oz); 150m (164 yds)

Weight: DK/Light worsted

Clover Stitch

Using two or three colours for the Clover Stitch leads to many possibilities, but the combination of turquoise, blue and lilac (C3) shows it to the best effect. The technique used to make this square is shown on page 27.

C1

Three warp layers in
8398 Navy
Weave in 9420
Como Blue

Warp

Weave

C2

Three warp layers in
7808 Purple Hyacinth
Weave in 7827
Goldenrod

Warp

Weave

C3

Two warp layers in
8398 Navy
Third warp layer in
9420 Como Blue
Weave in 7808
Purple Hyacinth

Warp

Weave

C4

Two warp layers in
7808 Purple Hyacinth
Third warp layer in
7827 Goldenrod
Weave in 9420
Como Blue

Warp

Weave

Basketweave Stitch

Using two or three colours for the Basketweave Stitch brings different effects.
Two colours create a simple contrasting design, while a third adds highlights. The
technique used to make this square is shown on page 45.

D1

Two warp layers in
8398 Navy
Weave in 9420
Como Blue

Warp

Weave

D2

Two warp layers in
7808 Purple Hyacinth
Weave in 7827
Goldenrod

Warp

Weave

D3

One warp layer in
8398 Navy
Second warp layer in
9420 Como Blue
Weave in 7808
Purple Hyacinth

Warp

Weave

D4

One warp layer in
7808 Purple Hyacinth
Second warp layer in
7827 Goldenrod
Weave in 9420
Como Blue

Warp

Weave

The Power of Contrasts

This combination uses two colours and one tone change. It can be used to create squares with a low or high contrast, which gives a very interesting result. Cascade Yarns Alpaca Lana D'Oro yarn works well on the pin loom for both the two- and three-layer warp thread techniques. The result is always a fabric that drapes well.

Yarns Used

Cascade Yarns Alpaca Lana D'Oro in 1124 Deep Teal, 1112 Pumpkin, 1048 Ochre, 1094 Intense Aqua
Fibre: 50% alpaca/50% wool; 100g (3½ oz); 200m (219 yds)
Weight: Aran/Worsted

Houndstooth Check Stitch

The pattern is enhanced when woven with contrasting colours and lost when using a low colour contrast, because it is defined by multiple details. Two colours are used for both warp and weave. The technique used to make this square is shown on page 46.

E1

Work in 1124 Deep Teal (colour 1) and 1094 Intense Aqua (colour 2)

Colour 1

Colour 2

E2

Work in 1112 Pumpkin (colour 1) and 1048 Ochre (colour 2)

Colour 1

Colour 2

E3

Work in 1094 Intense Aqua (colour 1) and 1112 Pumpkin (colour 2)

Colour 1

Colour 2

E4

Work in 1048 Ochre (colour 1) and 1124 Deep Teal (colour 2)

Colour 1

Colour 2

Double V Stitch

Combining two colours for the Double V Stitch results in a noticeable contrast, which is heightened when a third colour is added. The technique used to make this square is shown on page 31.

F1

Three warp layers in
1124 Deep Teal
Weave in 1094
Intense Aqua

Warp

Weave

F2

Three warp layers in
1112 Pumpkin
Weave in 1048 Ochre

Warp

Weave

F3

Two warp layers in
1124 Deep Teal
Third warp layer in
1094 Intense Aqua
Weave in 1112
Pumpkin

Warp

Weave

F4

Two warp layers in
1112 Pumpkin
Third warp layer in
1048 Ochre
Weave in 1094
Intense Aqua

Warp

Weave

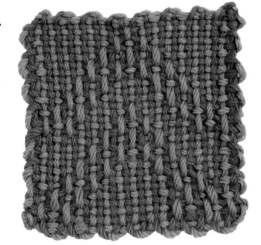

Different Contrasts

This example combines two tones of two colours: pink and blue. These colours can be combined to create low and high contrasts. Cascade Yarns Venezia Sport yarn is one of the thinnest recommended for weaving on a pin loom. When woven, it creates a silky fabric that should be used for decorative items as it is fragile and could disintegrate if subjected to heavy wear.

Yarns Used

Cascade Yarns Venezia Sport in 193 Powder Pink, 194 Cranberry, 130 Denim, 195 Deep Navy
Fibre: 70% merino wool/30% mulberry silk; 100g (3½ oz); 280m (307 yds)
Weight: DK/Light worsted

Basic Woven Stitch

The effect of the colour combinations in the Basic Woven Stitch is muted, whether the result is a low or a high contrast. The technique used to make this square is shown on page 26.

G1

Three warp layers in
193 Powder Pink
Weave in 194
Cranberry

Warp

Weave

G2

Three warp layers in
130 Denim
Weave in 195 Deep
Navy

Warp

Weave

G3

Two warp layers in
193 Powder Pink
Third warp layer in
194 Cranberry
Weave in 130 Denim

Warp

Weave

G4

Two warp layers in
130 Denim
Third warp layer in
195 Deep Navy
Weave in 194
Cranberry

Warp

Weave

Multiple Diamonds Stitch

The advantage of the Multiple Diamonds Stitch is that both two- and three-colour combinations result in dramatic contrasts. The technique used to make this square is shown on page 43.

H1

Two warp layers in
193 Powder Pink
Weave in 194
Cranberry

Warp

Weave

H2

Two warp layers in
130 Denim
Weave in 195 Deep
Navy

Warp

Weave

H3

One warp layer in
193 Powder Pink
Second warp layer in
194 Cranberry
Weave in 130 Denim

Warp

Weave

H4

One warp layer in
130 Denim
Second warp layer in
195 Deep Navy
Weave in 194
Cranberry

Warp

Weave

Earth
and Fire

This combination combines neutral
and earthy colours with fiery ones –
the former create a subtle contrast
that is balanced by the addition of the
fiery shade. The Cascade Yarns 220
Superwash Aran yarn is ideal for these
stitches and all the other three-warp
thread weaves.

Yarns Used

Cascade Yarns 220 Superwash Aran in
900 Charcoal, 822 Pumpkin, 1996
Melon, 875 Feather Gray,
819 Chocolate
Fibre: 100% superwash merino wool;
100g (3½ oz); 137.5m (150 yds)
Weight: Aran/Worsted

Diamond in Relief Stitch

Using two colours in Diamond in Relief Stitch works well, but only the addition of a high-contrast third colour accentuates the inner woven diamond. The technique used to make this square is shown on page 29.

I1

Three warp layers in
900 Charcoal
Weave in 822 Pumpkin

Warp

Weave

I2

Three warp layers in
875 Feather Gray
Weave in 819
Chocolate

Warp

Weave

I3

Two warp layers in
900 Charcoal
Third warp layer in
822 Pumpkin
Weave in 1996 Melon

Warp

Weave

I4

Two warp layers in
875 Feather Gray
Third warp layer in
819 Chocolate
Weave in 1996 Melon

Warp

Weave

Honeycomb Stitch

The Honeycomb Stitch is an ideal place to showcase a high-contrast third colour. The effect of a two-colour combination is more muted. The technique used to make this square is shown on page 35.

J1

Three warp layers in
900 Charcoal
Weave in 822 Pumpkin

Warp

Weave

J2

Three warp layers in
875 Feather Gray
Weave in 819
Chocolate

Warp

Weave

J3

Two warp layers in
900 Charcoal
Third warp layer in
822 Pumpkin
Weave in 1996 Melon

Warp

Weave

J4

Two warp layers in
875 Feather Gray
Third warp layer in
819 Chocolate
Weave in 1996 Melon

Warp

Weave

Cool Neutrals

Here a combination of cool and neutral colours create a contrast that is enhanced by the addition of the third cool colour. The thickness of the Cascade Yarns Baby Alpaca Chunky yarn is perfect for the pin loom – but any thicker and it would be difficult to wind the warp threads on the loom.

Yarns Used

Cascade Yarns Baby Alpaca Chunky in 602 Linen, 584 Colonial Blue Heather, 570 Charcoal, 612 Mystic Purple, 582 Sapphire Heather
Fibre: 100% baby alpaca; 100g (3½ oz); 98.8m (108 yds)
Weight: Chunky

Diamond Stitch

A contrast can be achieved using just two colours in the Diamond Stitch – in fact, if you add a third colour, the effect is lost and results in a completely different pattern. The technique used to make this square is shown on page 41.

K1

Two warp layers in 584 Colonial Blue Heather
Weave in 570 Charcoal

Warp

Weave

K2

Two warp layers in 602 Linen
Weave in 612 Mystic Purple

Warp

Weave

K3

One warp layer in 584 Colonial Blue Heather
Second warp layer in 570 Charcoal
Weave in 582 Sapphire Heather

Warp

Weave

K4

One warp layer in 602 Linen
Second warp layer in 612 Mystic Purple
Weave in 582 Sapphire Heather

Warp

Weave

Woven Edge Stitch

You can use two or three colours to achieve the contrast effect in the Woven Edge Stitch, although using three creates more movement in the pattern. The technique used to make this square is shown on page 30.

L1

Three warp layers in
584 Colonial Blue
Heather
Weave in 570 Charcoal

Warp

Weave

L2

Three warp layers in
602 Linen
Weave in 612 Mystic
Purple

Warp

Weave

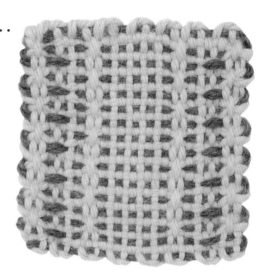

L3

Two warp layers in 584
Colonial Blue Heather
Third warp layer in
570 Charcoal
Weave in Sapphire
Heather

Warp

Weave

L4

Two warp layers in
602 Linen
Third warp layer in
612 Mystic Purple
Weave in Sapphire
Heather

Warp

Weave

Hot and Cold

A combination of two warm and two cool colours, each in two different levels of saturation, creates autumn-like tweed effects. The thickness of Cascade Yarns 220 Superwash Sport yarn is ideal for the pin loom and creates a loose, delicate fabric, especially when used with two-layer warp stitches.

Yarns Used

Cascade Yarns 220 Superwash Sport in 9593 Ginseng, 2401 Burgundy, 9451 Lake Chelan Heather, 8021 Beige
Fibre: 100% Peruvian Highland wool; 50g (1½ oz); 150m (164 yds)
Weight: DK/Light worsted

Arrow Stitch

An attractive tweed fabric can be created using two colours in Arrow Stitch. However, adding a third colour will create visually intriguing results. The technique used to make this square is shown on page 40.

M1

Two warp layers in
2401 Burgundy
Weave in 8021 Beige

Warp

Weave

M2

Two warp layers in
9593 Ginseng
Weave in 9451 Lake
Chelan Heather

Warp

Weave

M3

One warp layer in
2401 Burgundy
Second warp layer in
8021 Beige
Weave in 9593
Ginseng

Warp

Weave

M4

One warp layer in
9593 Ginseng
Second warp layer in
9451 Lake Chelan
Heather
Weave in 8021 Beige

Warp

Weave

Square in Relief Stitch

Two colours are ideal for the Square in Relief Stitch – add a third contrast shade and you have a different effect altogether. The technique used to make this square is shown on page 33.

N1

Three warp layers in
2401 Burgundy
Weave in 8021 Beige

Warp

Weave

N2

Three warp layers in
9593 Ginseng
Weave in 9451 Lake
Chelan Heather

Warp

Weave

N3

Two warp layers in
2401 Burgundy
Third warp layer in
8021 Beige
Weave in 9593
Ginseng

Warp

Weave

N4

Two warp layers in
9593 Ginseng
Third warp layer in
9451 Lake Chelan
Heather
Weave in 8021 Beige

Warp

Weave

Rustic Heathers

Two warm and two cool colours are used here to create rustic fabrics. The thickness of Cascade Yarns 220 Superwash Sport yarn creates a loose and delicate fabric, especially when using the two-layer warp method. Also the yarns are slightly variegated, giving the colour an extra depth. Added to this, the textured fibre will give a rustic look to the fabric.

Yarns Used

Cascade Yarns 220 Superwash Sport in 9459 Yakima Heather, 9454 Rainier Heather, 9566 Olive Oil, 9325 Westpoint Blue Heather
Fibre: 100% Peruvian Highland wool; 50g (1 oz); 150m (164 yds)
Weight: DK/Light worsted

X Stitch

Two colours work well together in the X Stitch – in fact, adding a third contrast will detract from the contrasts and lose the effect. The technique used to make this square is shown on page 42.

01

Two warp layers in 9459 Yakima Heather
Weave in 9566 Olive Oil

Warp

Weave

02

Two warp layers in 9454 Rainier Heather
Weave in 9325 Westpoint Blue Heather

Warp

Weave

03

One warp layer in 9459 Yakima Heather
Second warp layer in 9566 Olive Oil
Weave in 9454 Rainier Heather

Warp

Weave

04

One warp layer in 9454 Rainier Heather
Second warp layer in 9325 Westpoint Blue Heather
Weave in 9459 Yakima Heather

Warp

Weave

Diagonal Lines Stitch

You can use two or three colours for the Diagonal Lines Stitch: if you use two colours, the woven colour will stand out; if you use three, the third warp layer will stand out. The technique used to make this square is shown on page 34.

P1

Three warp layers in 9459 Yakima Heather
Weave in 9566 Olive Oil

Warp

Weave

P2

Three warp layers in 9454 Rainier Heather
Weave in 9325 Westpoint Blue Heather

Warp

Weave

P3

Two warp layers in 9459 Yakima Heather
Third warp layer in 9566 Olive Oil
Weave in 9454 Rainier Heather

Warp

Weave

P4

Two warp layers in 9454 Rainier Heather
Third warp layer in 9325 Westpoint Blue Heather
Weave in 9459 Yakima Heather

Warp

Weave

Jewel Brights

Five jewel-like colours of an equal saturation create a bright fabric ideal for children. The best ways to combine them are to use two colours that are similar in tone, or three that contrast with each other. To really make the patterns stand out, pick a colour with a high contrast. Weave two or even three strands of the Cascade Yarns Alpaca Lace yarn at a time, as they are quite thin. Two strands were used for these samples and the result was a soft, delicate fabric.

Yarns Used
Cascade Yarns Alpaca Lace in 1425 Provence, 1427 Pacific, 1428 Lime Heather, 1432 Sapphire Heather, 1407 Amethyst Heather
Fibre: 100% baby alpaca; 50g (1½ oz); 400m (437 yds)
Weight: Sock/Fingering

Volume Stitch

The best ways to combine these jewel-like colours are to use two that are similar in tone, or three that contrast with each other. Both work well with the Volume Stitch. The technique used to make this square is shown on page 28.

Q1

Three warp layers in
1428 Lime Heather
Weave in 1427 Pacific

Warp

Weave

Q2

Three warp layers in
1407 Amethyst Heather
Weave in 1432 Sapphire
Heather

Warp

Weave

Q3

Two warp layers in
1428 Lime Heather
Third warp layer in
1427 Pacific
Weave in 1425
Provence

Warp

Weave

Q4

Two warp layers in
1407 Amethyst Heather
Third warp layer in
1432 Sapphire Heather
Weave in 1425 Provence

Warp

Weave

Triangle in Relief Stitch

To really make the Triangle in Relief Stitch pattern stand out use two colours, one with a high contrast. Using a third colour creates a tweedy, less defined effect. The technique used to make this square is shown on page 33.

R1

Three warp layers in
1428 Lime Heather
Weave in 1427 Pacific

Warp

Weave

R2

Three warp layers in
1407 Amethyst Heather
Weave in 1432
Sapphire Heather

Warp

Weave

R3

Two warp layers in
1428 Lime Heather
Third warp layer in
1427 Pacific
Weave in 1425
Provence

Warp

Weave

R4

Two warp layers in
1407 Amethyst Heather
Third warp layer in
1432 Sapphire Heather
Weave in 1425
Provence

Warp

Weave

Rich Tones

This combination uses two cool colours and two warm ones to create a subtle background for a third colour, which adds contrast and movement. Cascade Yarns Venezia Worsted yarn is easy to weave on the pin loom and the resulting fabric is very soft to the touch.

Yarns Used

Cascade Yarns Venezia Worsted in 108 Autumn Walk, 150 Blue Velvet, 119 Cloudy Evening, 194 Cranberry
Fibre: 70% merino wool/30% mulberry silk; 100g (3½ oz); 199m (219 yds)
Weight: Aran/Worsted

Scottish Stitch

Using cool and warm colours for the Scottish Stitch creates the opportunity to create small areas of colour, especially when several squares are combined. The two colours are referred to as colours 1 and 2, to correspond with the sample shown on page 36. The technique used to make this square is shown on page 37.

S1

Work in 150 Blue Velvet (colour 1) and 119 Cloudy Evening (colour 2)

Colour 1

Colour 2

S2

Work in 194 Cranberry (colour 1) and 108 Autumn Walk (colour 2)

Colour 1

Colour 2

S3

Warp layer in 150 Blue Velvet and 119 Cloudy Evening Weave threads 1–8 with 150 Blue Velvet and 9–16 with 108 Autumn Walk

Warp

Weave

S4

Warp layer in 194 Cranberry and 108 Autumn Walk Weave threads 1–8 with 94 Cranberry and 9–16 with 150 Blue Velvet

Warp

Weave

Triple Zigzag Stitch

Depending on the colours used for each layer of the Triple Zigzag Stitch, different elements of the zigzags are highlighted. The technique used to make this square is shown on page 30.

T1

Three warp layers in
150 Blue Velvet
Weave in 119
Cloudy Evening

Warp

Weave

T2

Three warp layers in
194 Cranberry
Weave in 108
Autumn Walk

Warp

Weave

T3

Two warp layers in
150 Blue Velvet
Third warp layer in
119 Cloudy Evening
Weave in 108
Autumn Walk

Warp

Weave

T4

Two warp layers in
194 Cranberry
Third warp layer in
108 Autumn Walk
Weave in 150 Blue Velvet

Warp

Weave

High Contrasts

The effects created when a neutral colour is added to a combination of contrasting, saturated shades can be seen here. Three contrasting colours and one neutral are used. The thickness of Cascade Yarns 220 Superwash Aran yarn is ideal for three-warp layer stitches such as these – any thicker and it would be difficult to weave through.

Yarns Used

Cascade Yarns 220 Superwash Aran in 1946 Silver Gray, 1988 Red Plum, 811 Como Blue, 1989 Royal Purple
Fibre: 100% superwash merino wool; 100g (3½ oz); 137.5m (150 yds)
Weight: Aran/Worsted

Chain Stitch

In the Chain Stitch, the pattern works well with a combination of a neutral and a contrasting colour, but the results are more interesting when you combine three. They won't clash if they are all similar in tone. The technique used to make this square is shown on page 27.

U1

Three warp layers in 1946 Silver Gray
Weave in 1988 Red Plum

Warp

Weave

U2

Three warp layers in 811 Como Blue
Weave in 1989 Royal Purple

Warp

Weave

U3

Two warp layers in 1946 Silver Gray
Third warp layer in 1988 Red Plum
Weave in 811 Como Blue

Warp

Weave

U4

Two warp layers in 811 Como Blue
Third warp layer in 1989 Royal Purple
Weave in 1946 Silver Gray

Warp

Weave

Outlined X Stitch

Adding a third colour to the Outlined X Stitch makes little change to the pattern, but remember that whatever combination you choose, the woven yarn creates the cross. The technique used to make this square is shown on page 29.

V1

Three warp layers in
1946 Silver Gray
Weave in 1988
Red Plum

Warp

Weave

V2

Three warp layers in
811 Como Blue
Weave in 1989
Royal Purple

Warp

Weave

V3

Two warp layers in
1946 Silver Gray
Third warp layer in
1988 Red Plum
Weave in 811
Como Blue

Warp

Weave

V4

Two warp layers in
811 Como Blue
Third warp layer in
1989 Royal Purple
Weave in 1946
Silver Gray

Warp

Weave

Novelty Yarns

Unusual yarns spun to create a textured finish, raffia, string and other fibres, can all be used to create eye-catching fabrics. If you want to try to weave using a fragile yarn (or yarn substitute) use it for the warp threads and then something more robust – but fine – for weft weaving. These are more likely to withstand being pulled through the wound threads.

Novelty Yarns

Yarn stores sell any number of unusual textured yarns as well as those with unusual finishes that are exciting to weave with. Here are some of my favourites, all woven using the Basic Woven Stitch shown on page 26.

Pompom yarn

Pompom yarns are designed to create a bobbly fabric when knitted. However, when you weave with them the finish is far more exciting – three-dimensional patches of raised bobbles against a background of woven threads.

Fur yarns

Yarns spun to create a fur finish can be woven to make a fabric with an exciting piled surface.

Satin ribbon

Thin satin ribbon (no more than 2mm ($1/8$ in.) wide) makes a fabric with a beautiful sheen. Take your time when threading and weaving the ribbon so that it sits flat on the loom at all times.

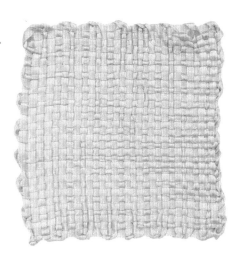

Elastic thread

Careful tensioning of the yarn is required if you plan to weave with an elastic thread. Do not stretch the elastic as you thread and weave it or the finished square will be uneven. The result is hardwearing and has some elasticity.

Pearlised acrylic thread

· ·

Work with two or three strands of thin, glossy thread to make a lightweight fabric ideal for scarves, jackets and other items that will not receive a lot of wear.

Metallic acrylic yarn

· ·

Weaving single threads of a thin yarn creates an airy fabric ideal for summer shawls or as decorative panels in a light evening jacket. The cloth will be fragile and ideal for adding decorative touches.

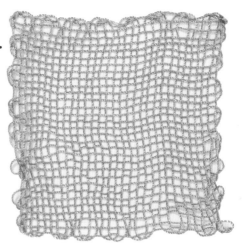

Textured metallic yarn

· ·

Single threads of these metallic yarns can be woven to create a lightweight fabric with a lovely drape. Their soft sheen makes them ideal for evening purses and delicate shawls.

Acrylic yarn with metallic highlights

· ·

The thin metallic thread spun into this acrylic yarn creates pretty highlights in the woven fabric. The result is substantial enough to be used for clothing and purses.

Coarsely spun cotton

In this sample, two neutral shades of a coarsely spun cotton have been threaded and woven together to create a lightweight summer fabric.

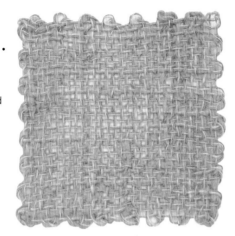

Sisal thread

Natural fibres such as sisal make an airy, rustic fabric ideal for home accessories such as place mats or coasters. It has no elasticity, so take care to get an even tension when threading the loom.

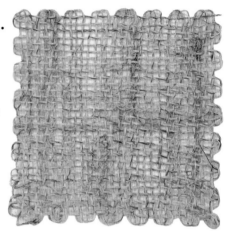

Chenille thread

A lightweight chenille thread works well on the Zoom Loom. The resulting fabric is velvety to the touch and perfect for clothing and warm scarves, hats and mittens.

Variegated cotton yarn

Using a variegated yarn is an easy way to create a colourful fabric. The designer has chosen the colours for you – all you have to do is weave. Choose a variegated yarn suitable for the item you want to make.

Creative Projects

Once you have mastered the art of weaving squares on the pin loom you will want to put them to good use. The fifteen beautiful projects in this section show different ways to assemble the squares, alternative construction and finishing techniques, and new colour combinations. You can substitute squares from the gallery for those used here, or use completely different yarn and colour combinations. Use these as a template for your own designs, or to spark ideas for projects of your own.

Wristbands

These mismatched wristbands make a fashion statement whether you make them in the calm, natural shades of the hand-painted cotton yarn shown here, or choose clashing brights.

Materials

Cascade Yarns Luna Paints (100% Peruvian tanguis cotton; 150m/ 164 yds); 100g/3½ oz; Aran/Worsted weight)

1 skein shade 9704 Sagebrush
1 skein shade 730 Sage
1 skein shade 738 Ecru
1 skein shade 703 Taupe
1 (2.5cm/1in) wooden button
5mm crochet hook
2 A squares in X Stitch (see page 42); use Sagebrush for the warp threads and Sage for the weft threads
2 B squares in X Stitch (see page 42); use Sagebrush for the warp threads and Ecru for the weft threads
2 C squares in X Stitch (see page 42); use Sagebrush for the warp threads and Taupe for the weft threads
2 D squares in Diagonal Stitch (see page 44); use Sage for the warp and weft threads

Skill Level: Easy

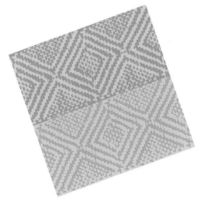

1 Sew together the A squares, using mattress stitch and making sure the woven pattern is consistent across the rows. Repeat with the C squares. Join the two rectangles together, making sure the woven pattern is consistent.

3 Work a single crochet border around the edges of the C squares using Taupe yarn. Sew the button in place on one side of the C section. Use three strands of Taupe yarn to create a loop for the button. The loop shown measures 3cm (1¼ in.) but choose a length to suit you. Weave in any loose ends.

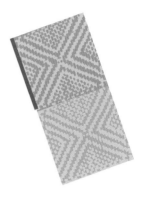

2 Fold the square in half and sew the A squares together as before to make a tube (shown in red on the diagram). Do not sew the C squares together.

4 Sew together the B squares along one edge using mattress stitch, making sure the woven pattern is consistent. Repeat with the D squares. Join the two rectangles together, making sure the weaves all face in the same direction. Fold the square in half and sew to make a tube. Fold back half of the D squares to make a cuff.

Fingerless Mittens

These chic fingerless gloves make the most of natural colours of an undyed yarn.
They have been designed to fit a small to medium woman's hand.

Materials

Cascade Yarns Eco Alpacas (100%
  baby alpaca; 100g/3½ oz; 200m/
  220 yds; Aran/Worsted weight)
1 skein shade 1517 Silver
1 skein shade 1524 Oatmeal
1 skein shade 1525 Silver Twist
5mm crochet hook
4 A squares in Arrow Stitch (see page
  40); use Silver for the warp and
  weft threads
4 B squares in Arrow Stitch (see page
  40); use Silver Twist for the warp
  threads and Silver for the weft threads
4 C squares in Arrow Stitch (see page
  40); use Silver Twist for the warp
  threads and Oatmeal for the weft
  threads

Skill Level: Intermediate

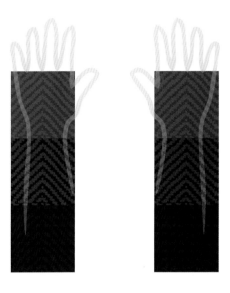

1 Arrange two sets of six squares as shown in the diagram.

2 Sew the squares together using mattress stitch. Fold each set in half vertically as shown in the diagram.

3 Use mattress stitch to sew the long, open sides together, leaving a 5cm (2 in.) gap for the thumbholes. The purple lines on the diagram show the seam lines (left).

4 Use Oatmeal to work a single crochet border around the thumbholes to reinforce them. Weave in any loose ends.

Infinity Scarf

This richly coloured infinity scarf can be worn loose around the neck, or wrapped around a couple of times for extra warmth.

Materials

Cascade 220 Superwash Aran (100% superwash merino wool; 100g/ 3½ oz; 137.5m/150 yds; Aran/Worsted weight)

1 skein shade 1427 Pacific

1 skein shade 1429 Icelander

1 skein shade 1428 Lime Heather

Note: All yarns are doubled throughout.

15 A squares in Basic Woven Stitch (see page 26); use Icelander for the warp threads and Pacific for the weft threads

15 B squares in Basic Woven Stitch (see page 26); use Lime Heather for the warp threads and Icelander for the weft threads

15 C squares in Basic Woven Stitch (see page 26); use Pacific for the warp threads and Lime Heather for the weft threads

15 D squares in Chain Stitch (see page 27); use Icelander for the warp threads and Pacific for the weft threads

15 E squares in Chain Stitch (see page 27); use Lime Heather for the warp threads and Icelander for the weft threads

15 F squares in Chain Stitch (see page 27); use Pacific for the warp threads and Lime Heather for the weft threads

Skill Level: Intermediate

1 Sew together each set of squares using mattress stitch so that you have six blocks three squares wide and five squares deep.

2 Sew the blocks together along the long sides using mattress stitch and in the following order: A, D, C, F, B, E.

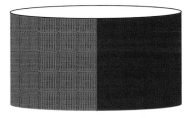

3 Stitch A and E together using mattress stitch to create a ring.

4 Fold the ring in half to create a double thickness of fabric two and a half squares deep and sew together along the open edge using whipstitch. Twist the ring so that the seam is hidden on the wrong side of the ring. Weave in any loose ends.

Hat

A cozy hat is essential – but one made from patterned woven squares makes a fashion statement as well. The hat has been designed to fit an average adult head and is 53cm (21 in.) in circumference.

Materials

Cascade Yarns Fixation (98.3% cotton, 1.7% elastic; 50g/1¾ oz; 91.4m/100 yds relaxed; DK/Light worsted weight)

1 skein shade 5860 Granny Smith Green

1 skein shade 5960 Sea Glass

1 skein shade 2319 Periwinkle

Note: The yarn contains elastic so be careful not to pull it any tighter than necessary when weaving the squares otherwise the finished hat will not have the elasticity required to make it fit well.

14 A squares in Multiple Diamonds Stitch (see page 43); use Granny Smith Green for the warp threads and Sea Glass for the weft threads

7 B squares in Diamond Stitch (see page 41); use Sea Glass for the warp and weft threads

Skill Level: Easy

1 Arrange the 14 A squares in two rows of seven, ensuring the weaves are parallel. Sew together using Granny Smith Green yarn and mattress stitch.

2 Sew the 7 B squares together to make a strip as before. Sew the strip to the base of the A-squares panel as before. Sew the two short ends together to make a ring.

3 Thread a needle with turquoise yarn and thread through the turquoise loops at the top of the hat. Pull the yarn as tightly as you can to gather the top of the hat, leaving as small a hole as possible. Tie together securely.

4 Use Periwinkle yarn to make a pompom 7cm (2¾ in.) in diameter and tie to the thread ends at the top of the hat. Weave in any loose ends.

Slippers

These cozy slippers are the perfect things to slip your feet into after a long day at work. They are designed to fit an adult woman's average shoe size. The design for one foot is a mirror image of the other foot.

Materials

Cascade Yarns Longwood (100% superwash extra-fine merino wool; 100g/3½ oz; 175m/191 yds; Aran/Worsted weight)

1 skein shade 19 Deep Ocean

1 skein shade 27 Lilac

1 skein shade 02 Gray Frost

2 buttons

5mm crochet hook

8 A squares in Volume Stitch (see page 28); use Gray Frost for the warp and weft threads

6 B squares in Volume Stitch (see page 28); use Lilac for the warp and weft threads

6 C squares in Volume Stitch (see page 28); use Deep Ocean for the warp and weft threads

Skill Level: Intermediate

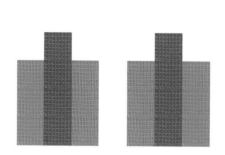

1 Arrange the squares as shown in the diagram and sew together using mattress stitch.

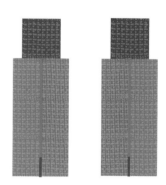

2 Fold the side edges together and sew as before (along the green line on the diagram), leaving half a square unsewn at one end (shown in red on the diagram).

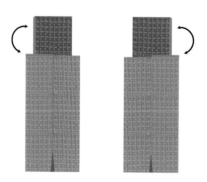

3 Turn the slippers so that the A squares are at the top, with a border of B and C on each side. Fold the unattached A squares to create a triangle and sew onto the C squares. Decorate the points with a button.

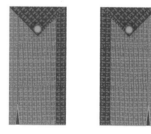

4 Work a single crochet border along the open edge of the slippers (shown in orange on the diagram) to reinforce and decorate them. Weave in any loose ends.

Poncho

This simple poncho is designed to flow loosely from the shoulders. The two symmetrical sections form a mirror image so take care to position the squares in a consistent direction. The pattern is designed to fit UK women's sizes 12–16.

Materials

Cascade Yarns Ecological Wool (100% natural Peruvian wool; 250g/9 oz; 437/478 yds; Chunky weight)
1 skein shade 8019 Antique
1 skein shade 0958 Cinnamon
5mm crochet hook
84 A squares in Diamond Stitch (see page 41); use Antique for the warp and weft threads
28 B squares in Diamond Stitch (see page 41); use Antique for the warp threads and Cinnamon for the weft threads

Skill Level: Intermediate

1 Assemble 14 rows of (from left to right) three A squares and one B square. Sew the squares together using mattress stitch.

2 Assemble and sew together the right-hand side so that it is a mirror image of the left.

3 Sew the two sections together along the B squares using whip stitch, leaving the centre six squares unsewn, as shown in the diagram. Weave in any loose ends.

4 Plait or crochet lengths of cord to create a belt. The sample in the photograph used both colours of yarn to create plaits of different thicknesses for a rustic finish.

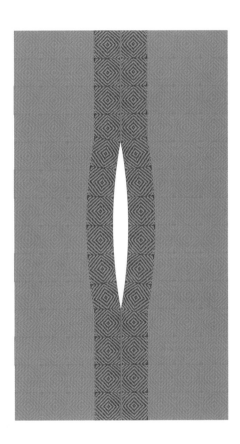

Sweater

This short-sleeved sweater uses subtle colour changes to create an elegant garment ideal for cool spring days. An elegant silk yarn creates drape and warmth. It is designed to fit UK women's sizes 12–16.

Materials

Cascade Yarns Heritage Silk (85% merino superwash wool, 15% mulberry silk; 100g/3½ oz; 400m/ 437 yds; Sock/Fingering weight)

2 skeins shade 5608 Pine

3 skeins shade 9817 Waterlilies

1 skein shade 5673 Lilac

Note: All yarns are doubled throughout.

20 A squares in Diagonal Stitch (see page 44); use Pine double for warp and weft threads

48 B squares in Basic Woven Stitch (see page 26); use Waterlilies double for warp and weft threads

12 C squares in Clover Stitch (see page 27); use Waterlilies double for the warp threads and Lilac double for the weft threads

Skill Level: Advanced

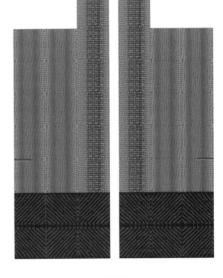

1 For the front left-hand side, arrange ten B squares, six C squares and six A squares as shown in the diagram, with the woven patterns all facing in the same direction. Use mattress stitch to sew all the squares together, except for the seam between the bottom two B squares on the left-hand side (marked in red on the diagram). Create the front right-hand side as a mirror image of the left. Each half uses a total of 22 squares.

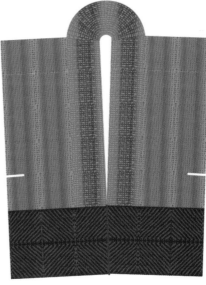

2 Sew together the two C squares at the top to create the collar and the A squares at the hem using mattress stitch to create the front of the sweater.

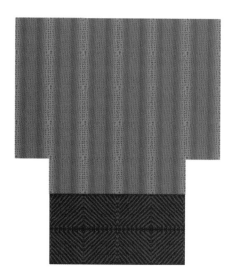

3 To create the back, arrange the remaining B and A squares as shown in the diagram, with the woven patterns all facing in the same direction, and sew together. You will need a total of 36 squares.

4 Place the back and front, with right sides together, and sew along the shoulders and collar. Next, sew the side seams below the sleeves. Finally, sew the sleeves together, stitching the cuff section only on the front, but the whole sleeve on the back, as shown on the diagram, right, in blue.

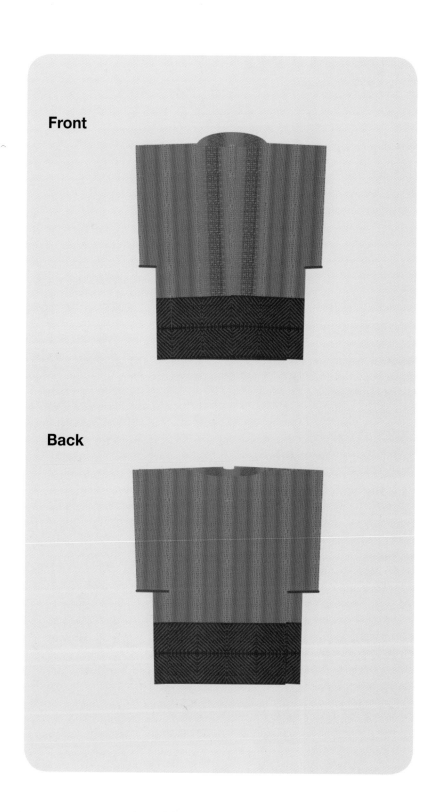

Front

Back

Dog's Coat

This cute coat is the perfect size for a small dog, such as a dachshund or border terrier. It covers the dog's back and features two sleeves for the front legs.

Materials

Cascade Yarns 220 Superwash Aran
  (100% superwash merino wool;
  100g/3½ oz; 137.5m/150 yds; Aran/
  Worsted weight)
1 skein shade 821 Daffodil
1 skein shade 822 Pumpkin
1 skein shade 1996 Melon
5mm crochet hook
9 A squares in Diagonal Stitch
  (see page 44); use Pumpkin for
  the warp threads and Melon for the
  weft threads
9 E squares in Houndstooth Check
  Stitch (see page 46); use Pumpkin for
  colour 1 and Daffodil for colour 2

Skill Level: Intermediate

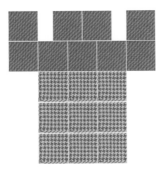

1 Assemble the squares as shown in the diagram and sew together using mattress stitch.

2 Fold the leg sections in half, with right sides facing, and stitch the long seams to make a tube using mattress stitch. Turn right-side out and fold up the bottom edge to make a turnover.

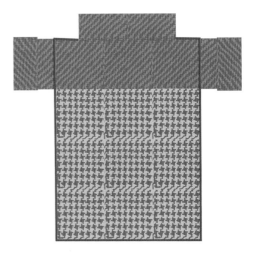

3 Work a single crochet border around the edge of the coat (shown in blue on the diagram). As well as giving a neat finish, this will reinforce the top of the sleeves for the front legs. Weave in any loose ends.

Hairband

A soft silk yarn makes a luxurious headband that can be dressed up for parties or dressed down for everyday wear. The sample shown is 58cm (23 in.) in circumference – ideal for an average adult head.

Materials

Cascade Heritage Silk (85% merino superwash wool, 15% mulberry silk; 100g/3½ oz); 400m/437 yds; Sock/ Fingering weight)

1 skein shade 5630 Aqua Foam

1 skein shade 5626 Turquoise

7 squares in Basic Three-layer Weave (see page 26); use Aqua Foam for the warp threads and Turquoise, used double, for the weft threads

Skill Level: Easy

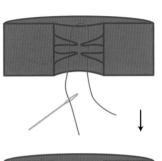

1 Arrange six of the squares side by side with the warp threads lying horizontally and aligned. Sew them together using Aqua Foam yarn and mattress stitch. Then sew the two ends together to make a ring.

2 Gather one of the squares by making three horizontal folds in it. Secure the gathers by running a length of yarn through them with a needle and then tie the ends together in a knot to secure.

3 Fold the remaining square over the gathers so that the warp threads are aligned and the top and bottom edges meet at the rear. Sew the top and bottom edges together, keeping the seam at the back of the headband.

4 Turn the square inside out and ensure the gathered edges at each side are even.

Gadget Cases

Keep your gadgets free from scratches by weaving a set of coordinating cases for them. The samples shown fit a tablet measuring 13 x 20cm (5 x 8 in.) and a laptop measuring 22.5 x 33cm (9 x 13 in.), but you can adjust the designs to fit other devices by using more – or fewer – woven squares.

Materials

Cascade Yarns Venezia Sport (70% merino wool, 30% mulberry silk; 100g/3½ oz; 281m/307.5 yds; DK/ Light worsted weight)

For the Tablet Case

1 skein shade 208 Citrus Cream

1 skein shade 101 White Heaven

1 skein shade 108 Autumn Walk

2 A squares in Honeycomb Stitch (see page 35); use Autumn Walk for the warp and weft threads

10 B squares in Honeycomb Stitch (see page 35); use Citrus Cream for the warp threads and White Heaven for the weft threads

For the Laptop Case

1 skein shade 208 Citrus Cream

1 skein shade 132 Mouse

4 buttons

24 C squares in Honeycomb Stitch (see page 35); use Citrus Cream for the warp threads and Mouse for the weft threads

Skill Level: Intermediate

1 For the Tablet Case, arrange the A and B squares as shown in the diagram, with two columns of six squares with the two A squares side by side. Sew together using mattress stitch.

2 Fold the B section in half horizontally to create the case and sew along the vertical sides using mattress stitch.

3 Fold over the A section to create a flap. Weave in any loose ends.

1 For the Laptop Case, arrange the 24 C squares into a rectangle three squares deep and eight squares wide. Sew the squares together using mattress stitch.

2 Fold the rectangle in half so the sides measure four squares wide. Sew along the base and open side using mattress stitch.

3 Reinforce the open edge of the cover by working three rows of single crochet around it using Mouse.

4 Decorate the open edge by sewing on buttons. If you want to be able to close the case, crochet chain loops to fit the buttons.

Lampshade

Neutral colours create a modern lampshade enhanced by the texture of the woven stitches. This elegant lampshade fits a shade 76cm (30 in.) in circumference and 20cm (8 in.) deep, but as the finished size of the squares depends on the yarn used and tension of the weave, check the dimensions of your squares before you start to assemble them.

Materials

Cascade Yarns Ultra Pima
  (100% Pima cotton; 100g/3½ oz;
  200m/220 yds; Light worsted/
  DK weight)
1 skein shade 3759 Taupe
1 skein shade 3798 Suede
1 skein shade 3718 Natural
Lampshade 76cm (30 in.) in
  circumference and 20cm (8 in.) tall
Glue
8 P1 squares in Diagonal Lines Stitch
  (see page 34); use Taupe for the
  warp threads and Natural for the
  weft threads
8 P3 squares in Diagonal Lines Stitch
  (see page 34); use Suede for the
  warp threads and Natural for the
  weft threads

Skill Level: Easy

1 Arrange eight squares in the following order: A, B, A, B, A, B, A, B.

2 Repeat Step 1, arranging the squares in the following order: B, A, B, A, B, A, B, A.

3 Sew the squares together as shown in the diagram, sewing the red seams before the green seams. Use mattress stitch and sew the squares together with the right sides facing you.

4 Sew the two short ends together to create a ring and weave in the loose ends. Work a single crochet seam. Position the ring over the lampshade and fold the top and bottom edges to the inside of the shade. Glue in place.

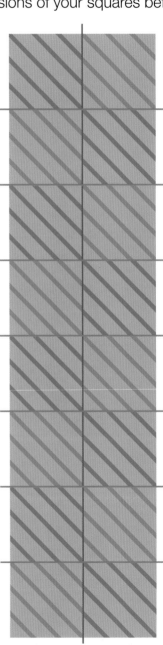

Tote Bag

This handy purse has a useful shoulder strap and flap closure. The wool and silk yarn is luxurious yet hardwearing – making it perfect for daily use.

Materials

Cascade Yarns Venezia Sport (70% merino wool, 30% mulberry silk; 100g/3½ oz; 281m/307.5 yds; DK/ Light worsted weight)

1 skein shade 5660 Gray
1 skein shade 5639 Olive
1 skein shade 5642 Blood Orange
1 skein shade 5641 Mango
Fabric to reinforce the strap (optional)
2 buttons and/or hook-and-loop fastener

Note: All yarns are doubled throughout.

12 A squares in Scottish Stitch (see page 36); use Gray for colour 1, Blood Orange for colour 2, and weave the second half (rows 9–16) with Mango

12 B squares in Basic Woven Stitch (see page 26); use Blood Orange for the warp threads and Olive for the weft threads

Skill Level: Intermediate

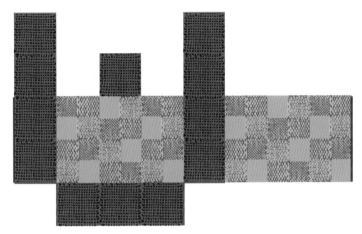

1 Assemble the 24 squares as shown in the diagram, then sew them together using mattress stitch and Blood Orange yarn.

2 Sew together the sides (shown in blue on the diagram), base (shown in purple), and strap (green) as before.

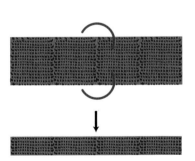

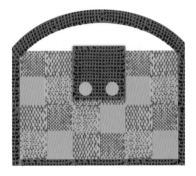

3 Fold the strap in half lengthwise and stitch the raw edges together so the seam is hidden on the inside of the strap. If you like, you can reinforce the handle with a piece of fabric. Weave in any loose ends.

4 Sew two buttons to the top of the bag, under the flap. Use your fingers to open up the woven squares to create buttonholes. Alternatively, use the buttons for decoration and sew a hook-and-loop fastener to the bag and the underside of the flap.

Materials

Cascade Yarns Highland Duo
  (70% baby alpaca, 30% merino wool;
  100g/3½ oz; 180m/197 yds; Aran/
  Worsted weight)
2 skeins shade 2204 Ecru
2 skeins shade 2303 Gray
2 skeins shade 2202 Latte
2 skeins shade 2317 Marine
2 skeins shade 2322 Loden
5mm crochet hook
17 A squares in Basic Woven Stitch
  (see page 26); use Ecru for the warp
  and weft threads
16 B squares in Basic Woven Stitch
  (see page 26); use Gray for the warp
  and weft threads
16 C squares in Basic Woven Stitch
  (see page 26); use Latte for the warp
  and weft threads
17 D squares in Basic Woven Stitch
  (see page 26); use Marine for the warp
  and weft threads
16 E squares in Basic Woven Stitch
  (see page 26); use Loden for the warp
  and weft threads
17 F squares in Square in Relief Stitch
  (see page 33); use Ecru for the warp
  threads and Loden for the weft threads
17 G squares in Square in Relief Stitch
  (see page 33); use Gray for the warp
  threads and Marine for the weft threads

Throw

Bring a warm glow to a chilly evening by wrapping yourself up in this classic throw. The squares are stitched together like a patchwork quilt to make a throw measuring 110 x 150cm (43 x 59 in.).

17 H squares in Square in Relief Stitch (see page 33); use Latte for the warp threads and Ecru for the weft threads

17 I squares in Square in Relief Stitch (see page 33); use Marine for the warp threads and Latte for the weft threads

17 J squares in Square in Relief Stitch (see page 33); use Loden for the warp threads and Gray for the weft threads

Skill Level: Intermediate

1 Assemble the squares as shown in the diagram to create 15 rows of 11 squares. You may find it helpful to use safety pins to join them together.

2 Sew the squares together using mattress stitch.

3 Using one of the yarns used for the squares, work a border of two rows of crochet slip stitch around the edges of the throw to create a neat finish. Weave in any loose ends.

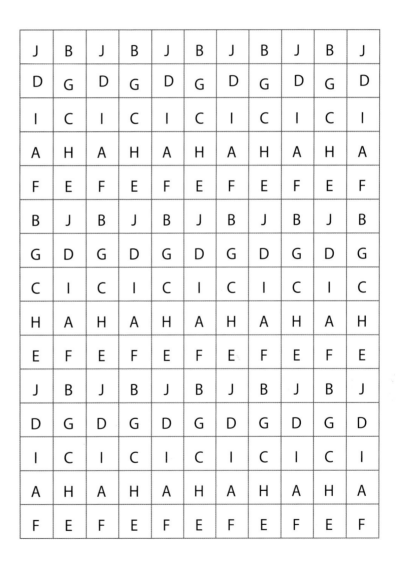

J	B	J	B	J	B	J	B	J	B	J
D	G	D	G	D	G	D	G	D	G	D
I	C	I	C	I	C	I	C	I	C	I
A	H	A	H	A	H	A	H	A	H	A
F	E	F	E	F	E	F	E	F	E	F
B	J	B	J	B	J	B	J	B	J	B
G	D	G	D	G	D	G	D	G	D	G
C	I	C	I	C	I	C	I	C	I	C
H	A	H	A	H	A	H	A	H	A	H
E	F	E	F	E	F	E	F	E	F	E
J	B	J	B	J	B	J	B	J	B	J
D	G	D	G	D	G	D	G	D	G	D
I	C	I	C	I	C	I	C	I	C	I
A	H	A	H	A	H	A	H	A	H	A
F	E	F	E	F	E	F	E	F	E	F

Pillow

Simple yarn tassels decorate the flap of this colourful pillow. Use this basic design to create larger pillows, rectangular pillows, or assemble them to make a square one.

Materials

Cascade Yarns Ultra Pima (100% pima
    cotton; 100g/3½ oz; 200m/220 yds;
    DK/Light worsted weight)
1 skein shade 3798 Suede
1 skein shade 3777 African Violet
1 skein shade 3747 Gold
Pillow pad 40 x 25cm (15 x 9 in.)
18 A squares in Double V Stitch (see
    page 31); use Suede for the warp
    threads and African Violet for the weft
    threads
4 B squares in Double V Stitch (see
    page 31); use Gold for the warp
    threads and Suede for the weft
    threads
2 C squares in Double V Stitch (see
    page 31); use African Violet for the
    warp threads and Suede for the weft
    threads

Skill Level: Intermediate

1 Assemble the squares as shown in the diagram and sew them together using mattress stitch.

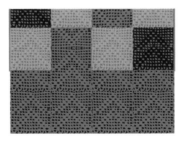

3 Fold over the top one and a half squares so that the right sides of the fabric face each other. Stitch the side edges (shown in green on the diagram) to create a flap. Weave in any loose ends. Insert the pillow pad.

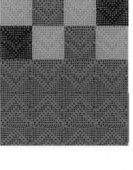

2 Fold over the bottom one and a half squares so that the right sides of the fabric face each other. Stitch the side edges (shown in green on the diagram).

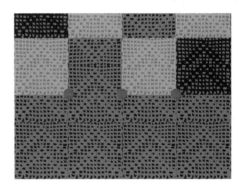

4 Cut seven (12.5cm/5 in.) lengths of Suede yarn and two (12.5cm/5 in.) lengths of Gold yarn. Use a needle to thread the lengths of yarn through a point where two squares meet at the edge of the flap (indicated in red on the diagram) and tie together to make a tassel. Repeat at the edge of the other two seams on the flap, three times in total.

Floor Cushion

This comfortable floor cushion is the perfect perch when you want to curl up with a book or catch up with your favourite TV show. The squares are joined together to make a square pillow 60cm (24 in.) square and 33cm (13 in.) deep.

Materials

Cascade Heritage 150
  (75% superwash merino wool,
  25% nylon; 150g/5½ oz;
  450m/492 yds; sport weight)
1 skein shade 5607 Red
1 skein shade 5606 Burgundy
1 skein shade 5633 Italian Plum
1 skein shade 5605 Plum
Cushion measuring 60 x 60 x 33cm
  (24 x 24 x 13 in.)
20 A squares in Triangle in Relief
  Stitch (see page 33); use Red for
  the warp threads and Plum for the
  weft threads
20 B squares in Triangle in Relief
  Stitch (see page 33); use Red for
  the warp threads and Italian Plum for
  the weft threads
50 C squares in Triangle in Relief
  Stitch (see page 33); use Red for
  the warp threads and Burgundy for
  the weft threads

Skill Level: Intermediate

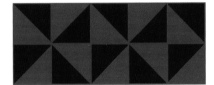

1 To create sides 1 and 3, assemble two sets of ten B squares to create a pinwheel effect as shown in the diagram.

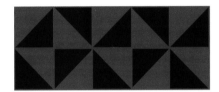

2 To create sides 2 and 4 of the cushion, assemble two sets of ten A squares to create a pinwheel effect as shown in the diagram.

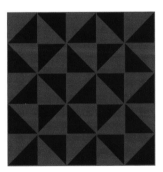

3 To create the top and bottom of the cushion, assemble two sets of 25 C squares to create a pinwheel effect as shown in the diagram.

4 Sew together the sides, top and bottom as shown in the diagram. Sew sides 1 and 3 to the top and bottom, and insert the cushion. Sew the remaining seams.

Resources

Looms

The Zoom Loom is available in most craft stores. Many models of hand-held loom are readily available online.

Zoom Loom

Schacht Spindle Company, Inc
6101 Ben Place
Boulder, CO 80301
Tel: +1 303 442 3212
info@schachtspindle.com
www.schachtspindle.com

Handmade Wooden Looms

Hazel Rose Looms
Rt. 2 Box 4792
Trinity Center, CA 96091
dorleska@tds.net
www.hazelroselooms.com

Vintage Looms

These can be found in vintage and charity shops, and online auction sites.

General Resources

eLoomination
www.eloomination.com

Carole's Crafts
Unit 3 Applied House
Fitzherbert Spur
Farlington, Hampshire, PO6 1TT
Tel: +44 (0)2392 318097
www.carolescraftsuk.co.uk

The Threshing Barn
Mill 2, Unit 3, Farfield Mill
Garsdale Road
Cumbria, Sedbergh, LA10 5LW
Tel: +44 (0)15396 20474
www.threshingbarn.com

Wild Fibres
Studio I-135, The Custard Factory
Gibb St, Birmingham B9 4AA
Tel: +44 (0)7979 770865
www.wildfibres.co.uk
www.wildcolours.co.uk

Yarns

Cascade Yarns

PO Box 58168
Tukwila, WA 98138
www.cascadeyarns.com

Cascade Yarns used in this book:

128 Superwash Aran

Chunky weight
100% superwash merino wool;
100g (3½ oz); 117m (128 yds)

220 Superwash Aran

Worsted or Aran weight
100% superwash merino wool;
100g (3½ oz); 137.5m (150 yds)

220 Superwash Sport

Light worsted or DK weight
100% Peruvian Highland wool;
50g (1¾ oz); 150m (164 yds)

Alpaca Lace

Sock or Fingering weight
100% baby alpaca; 50g (1¾ oz);
400m (437 yds)

Alpaca Lana D'Oro
Worsted or Aran weight; 50% alpaca, 50% wool; 100g (3½ oz); 200m (219 yds)

Baby Alpaca Chunky
Chunky weight
100% baby alpaca; 100g (3½ oz); 98.8m (108 yds)

Eco Alpaca
Worsted or Aran weight
100% baby alpaca; 100g (3½ oz); 200m (220 yds)

Ecological Wool
Chunky weight
100% natural Peruvian wool; 250g (9 oz); 437m (478 yds)

Fixation
Light worsted or DK weight
98.3% cotton, 1.7% elastic; 50g (1¾ oz); 91.4m (100 yds) relaxed

Heritage 150
Sport weight
75% superwash merino wool, 25% nylon; 150g (5½ oz); 450m (492 yds)

Heritage Silk
Sock or Fingering weight
85% merino superwash wool, 15% mulberry silk; 100g (3½ oz); 400m (437 yds)

Highland Duo
Worsted or Aran weight
70% baby alpaca, 30% merino wool; 100g (3½ oz); 180m (197 yds)

Longwood
Worsted or Aran weight
100% superwash extrafine merino wool; 100g (3½ oz); 175m (191 yds)

Luna Paints
Worsted or Aran weight
100% Peruvian tanguis cotton; 100g (3½ oz); 150m (164 yds)

Ultra Pima
Light worsted or DK weight
100% pima cotton; 100g (3½ oz); 200m (220 yds)

Venezia Sport
Light worsted or DK weight
70% merino wool, 30% mulberry silk; 100g (3½ oz); 280m (307 yds)

Venezia Worsted
Worsted or Aran weight
70% merino wool, 30% mulberry silk; 100g (3½ oz); 199m (219 yds)

Index

Acknowledgements

The author and publisher would like to thank Cascade Yarns for its generous help with providing a superb selection of yarns, used throughout this book.

The author and publisher would also like to thank the Schacht Spindle Company, Inc for providing the Zoom Looms used in this book. Check out the Schacht website for weaving tutorials and more great Zoom Loom project ideas. See page 140 for details.

The publisher would like to thank Simon Pask for his splendid photography of the squares and techniques, and Osvaldo Faúndez for his lovely project photography.

The publisher would also like to thank Emma Brace, Catherine Embleton and Sophie Scott for their help pattern checking and evaluating this book.

The author would like to thank everyone who helped make the squares and projects. Her weaving team: Gisela Pérez, Inés Correa, Verónica Ferreira, Ruby Arenas and Solange Clement; photographer Osvaldo Faúndez; photographic studio owner Carolina Correa; and models Amalia Infante, Trinidad Campos and Melchor the dog.